JOYCE'S VOICES

Hugh Kenner

Joyce's Voices

University of California Press

Berkeley · Los Angeles · London

University of California Press
Berkeley and Los Angeles, California

University of California Press, Ltd.
London, England

Copyright © 1978 by
The Regents of the University of California

First Paperback Printing 1979
ISBN 0-520-03935-1
Library of Congress Catalog Card Number: 76-3887
Printed in the United States of America

1 2 3 4 5 6 7 8 9

For
August Frugé

Contents

Prefatory

A correspondent from Missouri enquired: "In your book, *A Homemade World*, on page 155, you write, 'Joyce began *Ulysses* in naturalism and ended it in parody, understanding more profoundly than any of his followers that naturalism cannot end anywhere else, and a law like the hidden law that governs the unfolding of styles in *Ulysses* brought Hemingway to self-parody at last, as though, not understanding the history disclosed by Joyce, he was condemned to repeat it.'

"Would you mind briefly explaining this sentence? . . ."

My reply promised this book, most of which is derived from the four T.S. Eliot Memorial Lectures I called *Objectivity and After* and delivered in May 1975 at the University of Kent at Canterbury, where the windows of the Great Hall of Eliot College frame a distant prospect of the towers of the cathedral. In the Chapter House near those towers the first performance of *Murder in the Cathedral* was rehearsed just forty years previously, and since *Murder in the Cathedral* bore on my theme, that view of the towers might have been framed to provide a visiting speaker with a trope. Eliot too had coopted such adventitious fact, when he dramatized in his playscript Becket's death for an audience who would sit not fifty yards from the place where Becket died. So had Joyce, staging the first scene of *Ulysses* atop a tower any Dublin reader would have known how to reach by tram.

Eliot, the sometime theorist of Experience and the Object of Knowledge, had ample reason to insist on that 1935 occasion that the martyrdom of Thomas Becket had been real and that a cult still validated it. By way of what he had called the Mythological Method, he was attempting an extended derivation from *Ulysses*, the book (then only twelve years old) which by his own influential account parallels verifiable fact with myth. His tactics repay attention. Borrowing a form Gilbert Murray's translations had made fashionable, the Greek Tragedy with a Chorus, he boldly exploited what had been in Periclean times its central convention, that everyone sitting in the theater knew the unchanging myth, knew what must happen. It was probably the *Agamemnon* he had in mind, another play in which the principal character returns from abroad amid shrieking premonitions of doom, to be exhibited to an audience which knows he is about to be slaughtered.

Greek audiences did not see heroes killed, but Eliot's is so far a Christian play as to incorporate a ritual reenactment of the martyrdom which was itself a reenactment of Calvary. So the Canterbury audience sees Thomas killed. It is then immediately told that it does not know what it has seen. It is told this by the killers, who step forward with explanations; for instance that a first step has just been taken toward "a just subordination of the pretensions of the Church to the welfare of the State," or that Thomas, determined on death by martyrdom, had arranged a "Suicide while of Unsound Mind."

These summaries correspond to possible plays about the murder of Becket. How Eliot ensured that his own play would not be confused with either of them is another subject; suffice it to observe that he did not think he had done enough when he put the happenings before us. As one of the killers reminds us, we have all been eye-witnesses. In the theater we watch what happens. Yet whether Thomas has submitted to God's will, or whether he has elaborately killed himself, is not a question that attention to the evidential will qualify us to settle.

That men should learn to merely look and listen, that attention to what was and was not evidence might deliver the methodiz'd mind from self-deception, this was a doctrine of which much began to be heard in England not long after the Civil War. And though theaters are places to look and listen, what that doctrine portended for the stage was a rapid decline of prestige and of quality. The English theater had been a place for eloquence and declamation, and these grew suspect. What acquired prestige in their place was a new mode of literary art, eventually called fiction, in which the old conventions of a tale being told were gradually subdued to the new disciplines of evidence carefully marshalled. By the beginning of the nineteenth century the word "Objectivity" had begun to attach itself to such disciplines. By the beginning of the twentieth century the novel had been for a hundred years the literary genre *par excellence,* and Ibsen's enthusiasts had assimilated the theater itself to the novel's canons. All seemed to be moving on wheels toward a new enlightenment, presided over perhaps by Bernard

Shaw, whom Yeats claimed to have seen in a vision as
an incarnate sewing-machine, but a sewing-machine
that perpetually smiled.

And yet, just a quarter of the way into the new
century it was evident that the logic of any such evolu-
tion had collapsed. James Joyce, reputedly the supreme
exponent of a fiction subdued to scrupulous documen-
tation, had published *Ulysses*, which few could obtain
and fewer understand, and those who claimed to speak
of *Ulysses* with confidence were explaining that its details were ordered by a myth. A myth—it had been
myths that the discipline of objectivity had offered to
banish. Moreover, T. S. Eliot was explaining—in *The
Dial*, November 1923—that this use of myth had the
importance of a scientific discovery: the sort of bor-
rowed prestige Objectivity had once claimed. Eliot
himself was writing *Sweeney Agonistes*, the title of
which suggests how the mythological method hoped
to invade the theater itself. And though he did not
finish *Sweeney*, within ten years he had relied on the
method for a play he did finish, *Murder in the Cathedral*.

The whole story deserves careful looking into. As
the great age of twentieth-century Modernism re-
cedes, it grows increasingly clear that the decisive
English-language book of the century was *Ulysses*, the
first pivotal book in English since *Paradise Lost*. Its
example underlay *The Waste Land*, which terminated
Eliot's first poetic period. And it directed the decisive
reordering of the early *Cantos* which Pound undertook
early in the 1920's. Pound resisted, and Eliot as we shall
see passed over in silence, the fact that *Ulysses* commences in tacit adherence to the canons of naturalism,
of Objectivity, and then disorients readers by desert-
ing them, for reasons that have never been satisfactor-

ily explained. Its profusion of styles—what are we to make of *that*? If we can understand the apparent stylistic caprice that seems to invade and subvert Joyce's massive novel, we may hope for a radical understanding of numerous other matters pertaining to fiction, to language, to understanding itself—matters on which we should do well to be less intuitive than is customary. We shall understand better the century's poetic revolution as well: the redirection of verbal energies in which T. S. Eliot played a distinguished part.

I have drawn throughout on the talk of Fritz Senn and Brook Thomas and the letters of Adaline Glasheen. Mr. David Marshall prompted the sentences about Defoe. I am indebted to Mr. Henry Regnery for leave to re-use a few paragraphs from an essay I contributed to *Vive Vivas!* (1976), a Festschrift in honor of Eliseo Vivas. And I am indebted to Professor W. A. Whitehouse, Master of Eliot College, University of Kent, for the hospitality that distinguished my visit there.

Baltimore, 1976

1. Objectivity

When Eliot wrote "*Ulysses,* Order and Myth," which contains his famous pronouncement on the "mythological method," he was refuting Richard Aldington's finding that *Ulysses* was chaotic. In asserting that it was orderly, Eliot chose his ground with care. He concentrated on the Homeric parallel, which permitted a tidy adduction of order, and completely ignored what would strike anyone merely paging through the book, its stylistic variousness. This was feasible because neither Eliot nor Aldington was writing for readers who could page through the book, let alone try to master it; in neither the United States nor in England could *Ulysses* be legally obtained. All the early discussions have this curious property, that readers who had never seen a copy were required to assume Joyce's book was what the protagonist of the moment said it was. Controversy bore a curious resemblance to neo-classical wrangling about the merits and methods of lost Greek masterpieces. And if we knew *Ulysses* only from Eliot's remarks, as we know certain Greek works only from descriptions by Alexandrian commentators, we should have in our heads a paradigm almost unrecognizably different from the book Joyce wrote.

The book Eliot describes might have been written throughout in the prose of *Dubliners*. Its prose documents, he tells us, an "immense panorama of futility

and anarchy," much in need of control, of order, of
receiving "a shape and a significance." These qualities
the author had imparted with the aid of "a continuous
parallel between contemporaneity and antiquity." So
the "mythological method," which writers are now
free to use "instead of narrative method," constitutes
a grid on which to locate contemporary particulars,
observed with an objectivist's eye.

Save for myth, a "panorama of futility and anarchy"
would unroll through these pages, depicting the futile
and anarchic state of the modern world. This presupposes, without saying so, a responsiveness of mythless
writing to perceived fact for which the term "Objectivity" seems appropriate. Though it became an intellectual cause in England not long after the Civil
War, Objectivity, a sort of Royal Society rhetoric, did
not receive that name immediately. The *OED* editors
do not find the word in existence before 1803. "Em-
piricism" is a word with a longer pedigree; it was once
a pejorative term, primarily medical, used of physi-
cians who did not understand medicine but merely
used cures that had been observed to work. Well,
Lemuel Gulliver was apprenticed as a physician, and
we shall not find a better illustration of narrative controlled by the objective or empirical discipline than his
account of his first awakening in the kingdom of Lilliput, after a nine hours' sleep of exhaustion.

While he was sleeping, we remember, the little folk
of the realm had been busy tying him to the ground,
but that is not how the excellent Gulliver narrates it.
He is scrupulously faithful to what he observed, and to
the order in which he observed it. For first he opened
his eyes.

"It was just Day-Light. I attempted to rise, but was not able to stir: For as I happened to lie on my Back, I found my Arms and Legs were strongly fastened on each Side to the Ground; and my Hair, which was long and thick, tied down in the same Manner." This is what we have learned to regard as a natural narrative order: the effort to raise his shoulders has led to the discovery that his arms are immobilized; he tries to move his legs, and they are immobilized too; he tries to lift his head to see what is wrong, and only then discovers that his hair is fastened also. "I likewise felt several slender Ligatures across my Body, from my Armpits to my Thighs. I could only look upwards; the Sun began to grow hot, and the Light offended my Eyes. I heard a confused Noise about me, but in the Posture I lay, could see nothing except the Sky. In a little time I felt something alive moving on my left Leg, which advancing gently forward over my Breast, came almost up to my Chin; when bending my Eyes downward as much as I could, I perceived it to be a human Creature not six Inches high, with a Bow and Arrows in his Hands, and a Quiver at his Back." This is admirable in its self-control: something moving turns into a six-inch human only when it has marched into the restricted scope of Gulliver's vision, and not one clause sooner in the sentence.

That it is not over-ingenious of us to impute such discipline Swift himself assures us hereabouts in the text, by having Gulliver remark of one or two details that although he mentions them now he learned them later; also by inserting the careful phrase "as I conjectured" into the sentence where Gulliver, having seen one Lilliputian, states that he felt on his body the march of some forty more "of the same kind"; finally by drawing attention to the fact that pegs are not mentioned until they have been observed: "At length, struggling to get loose, I had the Fortune to break the Strings, and wrench out the Pegs that fastened my left Arm to the Ground; for, by lifting it up to my Face, I discovered the Methods they had taken to bind me."

Many words, we see, are being expended to apprise us that Gulliver is here responsive to a special discipline, which we may formulate: *We are told only the things an observer would have experienced, and told them in the order in which he would have experienced them.* Moreover, *Experience is equated with the discrete reports of the senses.*

This is Objectivity: the outer world conceived as a sequence of reports to someone's senses, and a sequence occurring in irreversible time. Swift does not seem to write this way out of habit, since to make a shrewd point he will suspend the discipline of Objectivity as often as it suits him; but he makes Gulliver write in this way, and can be rather emphatic about Gulliver's habitual scrupulousness in not getting ahead of himself.

For Swift is not interested in creating a canon of narrative; he is interested in a special idiosyncrasy of Gulliver's, which is to be aware of nothing but incremental evidence. Gulliver knows nothing until he has had an experience, and what he knows then is the trace of the experience he has had. This was for Swift, apparently, the hallmark of the new barbarism, this subjection of the mind to sequences of physical evidence, since it undid the revolution Socrates had effected in philosophy when he turned its attention wholly to moral questions. Socrates had rendered philosophy *useful*: moral determinations are useful, since they assist us to live. The discoveries which pertain to physical evidence are not useful at all, ministering as they do solely to idle curiosity (the distance of the earth from the sun in statute miles: who has a use for *that*?) So Gulliver's mind is busy in an idle way, like that of a Royal Society virtuoso, and it is no wonder that he is ultimately so helpless when talking horses challenge him to justify the ways of man to men.

Here the old usage of the word "empiric" is pertinent. Part of Swift's complicated game with Gulliver was to make him an empiric physician—not one who had grown learned in the art of medicine, but a forward fellow who had been apprenticed to a surgeon and watched how things were done. He then has Gulliver apply the empiric method to the whole conduct of his intellectual life, in a way we should find deliciously absurd. It was to articulate this fantastic procedure that Swift made much, here and there in the book, of a narrative method which bustles with ant-like tread from one crumb of experience to another, unambitious to encompass anything more.

This way of ordering details was to become, within two centuries, the paradigm of enlightened narrative, of vivid description, of all sophisticated literary, even poetic, presentation: as when Pound, working over the *Waste Land* drafts, underscored an Eliotic "perhaps" and wrote in the margin, "You, Tiresias, if you know, know damn well or else you don't." By then (1921) the enlightened writer determined the limits of a narrator's knowledge and permitted himself no blurring of those limits. This method is evidently close to that of the stage, where we see what we can see and nothing more.

It was a long time becoming the normative method
of fiction. It is not Dickens's method for instance.
Dickens brought his fictions vividly to life in dramatic readings before rapt audiences, and as Dickens
before an audience was playing Dickens—an impas-
sioned and impressionable sensibility moved to rage,
anguish, laughter, tears, despair by fictive doings and
sufferings—so Dickens at his writing-desk was doing
much the same thing, working himself into states we
cannot but share. Observe him at work in the second
chapter of *Oliver Twist*, stamping his sarcasms on
every phrase:

"Please, sir, I want some more."
The master was a fat, healthy man; but he turned very
pale. He gazed in stupefied astonishment on the small rebel
for some seconds, and then clung for support to the copper.
The assistants were paralysed with wonder; the boys with
fear.

"What!" said the master at length, in a faint voice.
"Please, Sir," replied Oliver, "I want some more."
The master aimed a blow at Oliver's head with the ladle;
pinioned him in his arms; and shrieked aloud for the beadle.

The board were sitting in solemn conclave, when Mr.
Bumble rushed into the room in great excitement, and ad-
dressing the gentleman in the high chair, said,

"Mr. Limbkins, I beg your pardon, Sir! Oliver Twist has
asked for more."

There was a general start. Horror was depicted on every
countenance.

"For *more*!" said Mr. Limbkins. "Compose yourself,
Bumble, and answer me distinctly. Do I understand that he
asked for more, after he had eaten the supper allotted by the
dietary?"

"He did, Sir," replied Bumble.

"That boy will be hung," said the gentleman in the white waistcoat. "I know that boy will be hung."

Though the ordering of incident and perception is scrupulously chronological, such writing is far from Objective; it is perpetually *judging*. Later we may remember what Oliver did, but as we read we are chiefly aware of what Dickens is doing: ensuring by his sarcasms that no reader will miss the frigid hypocrisy of beadle and board, or the mad conviction of officialdom that a law of nature has been violated. He has no passion left to spare for the pathos of Oliver, so enraged is he by the board. And if later we remember that scene as dominated by the tiny quaking indomitable orphan holding out his bowl, that is not a scene Dickens's writing holds before our attention, but one we construct with the aid of a memorable illustration.

That was written in 1838, in England. Fourteen years later, in France, Objectivity was achieving effects like the following:

"Stand up," said the teacher.

He stood up; the cap fell. The entire class began to laugh.

He stopped down and picked it up. His neighbor made it fall again by poking it with his elbow. He picked it up a second time.

"Get rid of your helmet," said the teacher, who was a witty man.

There was a burst of laughter from the students. It rattled the poor boy so much that he didn't know if he should keep the cap in his hand, leave it on the floor, or put it on his head. He sat down and placed it on his lap.

"Stand up," said the teacher, "and tell me your name."

The new boy stammered some unintelligible name.

"Once more!"

The same garbled syllables were heard, drowned by the hoots from the class.

"Louder," shouted the teacher, "louder!"

The new boy, now mustering up all his courage, opened an abnormally large mouth and, as if he were calling someone, shouted at the top of his voice the word, *Charbovari*.

It is not until the name Charles Bovary is later spelled out that anyone gets it straight; Flaubert is adhering to the Gulliverian principle that time has no forward loopings, and that an eyewitness—a schoolfellow of Charles's—will recount what he observed in the sequence in which he observed it. For this *is* an eyewitness account, as the account of Oliver asking for more is not. And if it is devoid of compassion, that is less because Charles's schoolfellow is no Dickens than because no objective eye could have discerned in the dumb ox of the schoolroom the tongue-tied romantic whose devotion will one day make a goddess out of silly Emma. This will be for the reader to perceive, and slowly; Objectivity eschews nudges.

Still, it is careful with evidence. We have seen young Charles Bovary through the eyes of a schoolfellow. Not many pages later we see Mademoiselle Rouault through the eyes of Charles, who as usual does not know what is happening to him. We may note that she is Mademoiselle Rouault when they commence a breakfast together after Charles has set her father's leg, and has become Mademoiselle Emma by perhaps half an hour later, which suggests that over their collation she volunteered a detail Charles wouldn't have asked her for. So she is a young lady who offers her name.

We sense Charles being more aware of her than he realizes: "As the room was chilly, she shivered a little while eating. This caused her full lips to part slightly. She had a habit of biting them when she wasn't talking." He has noticed that! He pays repeated visits, seeing to the leg, and his awareness increases.

She would always walk him back to the first step of the porch. If his horse had not yet been brought around, she would remain there. They had said good–bye to each other and were no longer chatting; the fresh air would envelope her, blowing the little wisps of hair on her nape in all directions, or moving over her hips the strings of her apron, which were twisting like streamers.

All this culminates in a vignette of diffuse sensuality.

One time during a thaw, moisture was trickling from the tree bark in the yard; the snow on the roofs of the buildings was melting. She stood on the threshold, then went to fetch her parasol and opened it. The sun came through the dove-colored silk parasol, its rays moving over the white skin of her face. She smiled beneath it at the mild warmth of the season, and you could hear the drops of water, one by one, falling on the taut-stretched silk.★

"You could hear" means "Charles heard"; the construction is impersonal because his normal torpidity is redoubled by his numb fascination with Emma, sunlight, melting snow and a parasol (a parasol! on that clod-hopping farm!) so that he is scarcely to be treated as a person. Later we learn that it took Emma's father, who had fiscal reasons for welcoming the match, fully

★Asterisks send you to notes at the back of the book; you may read them now, or later.

forty-nine minutes to persuade Emma into it. We have this fact because Charles keeps consulting his watch as he waits for a signal, and we are at liberty to deduce that Emma was slow to consent because she had more exalted notions of a husband, and to deduce moreover that Charles appears to deduce nothing whatsoever. "And so a wedding took place, to which forty-three people came and sat at the table for sixteen hours. It began again the next day and continued to a lesser extent the following days."

This is Objectivity, and it lays certain traps. Emma is vain and silly and headstrong, entangles herself in liaison after liaison, and kills herself when she can imagine no other finale. We are apt not to reflect how much of her fascination is imputed to her by herself, how much more by the dumb devotion of Charles, who himself is diminished both by Emma's scorn and by the cool objectivity of that first narrator, the schoolfellow.

The first victim of this circle of relativities was the Imperial Attorney, Mons. Ernest Pinard, who pronounced to a courtroom in 1857 the indictment against a book which contained, he said, no condemnation of what he called "this woman." "There is not one character in the book who might condemn her. If you find in it one good character, if you find in it one single principle by virtue of which the adulteress is stigmatized, I am wrong." The Imperial Attorney was by definition not wrong. "Christian morality stigmatizes realistic literature, not because it paints the passions—hatred, vengeance, love (the world only lives by these, and art must paint them)—but because it paints them without restraint, without bounds. Art without rules is no longer art. It is like a woman who throws off all garments."

The judge was not unpersuaded, and his verdict of acquittal may be paraphrased, "Not guilty by reason of inexperience." The author, it was judged, had been led astray by excess of technical zeal, and committed the fault "of forgetting that literature, like art, if it is to achieve the good work that is its mission to produce, must be chaste and pure in its form as in its expression."

Multiple illusion—that was the substance of Objectivity's rendering: mirror on mirror mirroring all the show. But Emma's sinfulness ought to have been made explicit. The trial of Flaubert is oddly like the last scene of *Murder in the Cathedral*, when the Knights step forward and seek to persuade us that what we have seen was not spiritually edifying at all: was either a headstrong cleric whose pretensions met their proper end, or a self-designated martyr who rushed on his slayers' swords in mistaken ecstasy.

Art, however, apparently improves, and by 1905 James Joyce had written "Grace," a story which would have caused the Imperial Attorney no disquiet whatever. This account of the reclamation of Tom Kernan commences with an act of disinterested charity—"Two gentlemen who were in the lavatory at the time tried to lift him up: but he was quite helpless"—and makes its way through a positive crescendo of edification to a sermon which it reports with helpful fullness, sharing with us the preacher's explication of a difficult but practical text. En route to the sermon it ventilates a religious discussion, in which four moral men refute their fallen brother's errors and encourage him to amend his life. Though they are not always perfectly informed (for instance the poet did not say "Great minds are very near to madness," though he said something fairly like it) still they tend to understand the main points to be made, as that, though some popes were admittedly "not exactly . . . you know . . . up to the knocker," still "not one of them ever preached *ex cathedra* a word of false doctrine. Now isn't that an astonishing thing?"

Objectivity is this story's discipline, its sequence of presentations faithful to the experience of an imagined spectator (the reader), its prose scrupulously neutral. The ironic sentence about Mrs. Kernan's devoutness—"Her faith was bounded by her kitchen, but, if she was put to it, she could believe also in the banshee and in the Holy Ghost"—may be cited as an exception, but Mrs. Kernan stays to one side of the story's main business.

And yet "Grace" is as subversive a story as *Dubliners* contains: the story against which Irish Catholic opinion should have expended its animus, instead of fussing about the word "bloody" and the naming of public houses. If it be asked in what way the story is not a tribute to the mysterious working of grace, we might commence an answer by noting its quiet but pervasive preoccupation with unsupernatural detail, notably with social nuance, beginning with the applicability of the word "gentleman." "Two gentlemen," the first sentence commences; and as for the man whose clothes are smeared with filth and ooze, "One of the curates said he had served the gentleman a small rum."

"Was he by himself?" asked the manager.
"No, sir. There was two gentlemen with him."

These aren't the two gentlemen in the lavatory but two boozers who have deemed it prudent to slip away; still, by the convention of the moment they are "gentlemen." Later it is judged that "The gentleman fell down the stairs," and his right to this title, despite his befouled condition, seems not unconnected with his possession of a silk hat. Indeed,

> Mr Kernan was a commercial traveller of the old school which believed in the dignity of its calling. He had never been seen in the city without a silk hat of some decency and a pair of gaiters. By grace of these two articles of clothing, he said, a man could always pass muster.

Here is the word "grace" hard by the word "believed," as though to record the normal Dublin sense of these words. For Tom Kernan, the religion he adopted just before his marriage is staffed by "ignorant, bumptious" clergy: hence the points his friends are careful to make in the middle part of the story. These include: that the Jesuits, "the grandest order in the Church," "cater for the upper classes"; that next Thursday's retreat is to be "for business men" and its Jesuit preacher "a man of the world like ourselves"; that Pope Leo XIII "was one of the most intellectual men in Europe," in fact wrote a Latin poem "on the invention of the photograph." And as promised, the Jesuit church fills with "gentlemen," "all well dressed and orderly," and these gentlemen see carefully to the knees of their trousers and to their hats. They include "Mr Fanning, the registration agent and mayor maker of the city" and "old Michael Grimes, the owner of three pawnbroker's shops," and they hear a text adapted for the guidance of "business and professional men," in fact men of the world. We can understand the rapturous decorum of our story's party of five, which includes one dilapidated tea-taster, one grocer of mod-

est achievements, and three minor civil servants of
whom one has a drunken wife and another a checkered
history of living by his wits.

So far, Objectivity has seemed to work with facts. In
the last few hundred words of "Grace," however, we
perceive as clearly as anywhere in *Ulysses* that it is
working with the resources of language. The effect is
impossible to miss. After many pages of dialogue we
are offered eloquence, and suddenly we are not hearing
the preacher's voice. The presentation is *oratio obliqua*:

> He told his hearers that he was there that evening for no
> terrifying, no extravagant purpose; but as a man of the
> world speaking to his fellow-men. He came to speak to
> business men and he would speak to them in a businesslike
> way. If he might use the metaphor, he said, he was their
> spiritual accountant . . . .

In its deadly frigidity, this expulses any reflection on
God's mysterious ways; the story's manner has grown
as cold as a Dublin church, and the source of its cold-
ness, we may suddenly reflect, is not the author but the
preacher, whose contrivance the author's stylistic contrivance obeys.

For nothing is as dependent as Objectivity on language and the rituals of language, Objectivity which
had promised to evade rhetoric and make the facts
effect their own declaration. Even the opening sentence of "Grace," it grows clear, was shaped by linguistic contrivance, a delicate oxymoron: "Two gentlemen who were in the lavatory at the time . . ." Joyce
has a way of ringing an opening sentence like a coin on
a counter; we respond to the ring; our sensors lock in.
And its right true ring proves to have been the ring of
lead.

2. The Uncle Charles Principle

The first sentence of "The Dead" has also a leaden ring, very perceptible to a translingual ear. (Joyce's household language was Italian, his public language during the *Ulysses* period successively Triestino, Schweizerdeutsch, and French. He was normally poised between some other language and English.)

Lily, the caretaker's daughter, was literally run off her feet.

Translate that into any alien tongue you like. "Literally?" To wonder what "literally" may mean is the fear of the Word and the beginning of reading. Whatever Lily was literally (Lily?) she was not literally run off her feet. She was (surely?) *figuratively* run off her feet, but according to a banal figure. And the figure is hers, the idiom: "literally" reflects not what the narrator would say (who is he?) but what Lily would say: "I am literally run off my feet." And sure enough, the paragraph goes on to designate the shabby crew who attend that party as the ladies and the gentlemen, which would be Lily's idiom likewise. Joyce is at his subtle game of specifying what pretensions to elegance are afoot on this occasion, and he does so with great economy by presenting a caretaker's daughter (Americans say 'the janitor's girl') cast for this evening as hall maid, and coping amid inconvenient facilities with too many simultaneous arrivals. "Hardly had she brought one gentleman into the little pantry behind the office on the ground floor and helped him off with his overcoat than the wheezy hall-door bell clanged again and she had to scamper along the bare hallway to let in another guest. It was well for her she had not to attend to the ladies also."

So that first sentence was written, as it were, from Lily's point of view, and though it looks like "objective" narration it is tinged with her idiom. It is Lily, not the austere author, whose habit it is to say "literally" when "figuratively" is meant, and the author is less recounting the front-hall doings than paraphrasing a recounting of hers.

This is a small instance of a general truth about Joyce's method, that his fictions tend not to have a detached narrator, though they seem to have. His words are in such delicate equilibrium, like the components of a sensitive piece of apparatus, that they detect the gravitational field of the nearest person. One reason the quiet little stories in *Dubliners* continue to fascinate is that the narrative point of view unobtrusively fluctuates. The illusion of dispassionate portrayal seems attended by an iridescence difficult to account for until we notice one person's sense of things inconspicuously giving place to another's. The grammar of twelve of the stories is that of third-person narrative, imparting a deceptive look of impersonal truth. The diction frequently tells a different tale.

Scanning *A Portrait of the Artist as a Young Man* fifty years ago, the eye of Wyndham Lewis was caught by what seemed an inadvertency of diction in a book not quite, as he thought, completely "swept and tidied":

Every morning, therefore, Uncle Charles repaired to his outhouse but not before he had greased and brushed scrupulously his back hair and brushed and put on his tall hat.

Lewis thought that in catching Joyce writing "repaired" he had caught him off guard. "People," he said, "*repair* to places in works of fiction of the humblest order." He was characterizing Joyce as a humble scrivener who kept himself from dropping into cliché by not wholly incessant vigilance. But the normal Joycean vigilance has not faltered here. Like the "literally" of the perhaps illiterate Lily, "repaired" wears invisible quotation marks. It would be Uncle Charles's own word should he chance to say what he was doing. Uncle Charles has notions of semantic elegance, akin to his ritual brushing of his hat; we hear him employing the word "salubrious," also the word "mollifying." If Uncle Charles spoke at all of his excursions to what he calls the outhouse,★ he would speak of "repairing" there.

Not that he does so speak, in our hearing. Rather, a speck of his characterizing vocabulary attends our sense of him. A word he need not even utter is there like a gnat in the air beside him, for us to perceive in the same field of attention in which we note how "scrupulously" he brushes his hat. This is apparently something new in fiction, the normally neutral narrative vocabulary pervaded by a little cloud of idioms which a character might use if he were managing the narrative. In Joyce's various extensions of this device we have one clue to the manifold styles of *Ulysses*; what is the first half of "Nausicaa," for instance, but Gerty Macdowell's very self and voice, caught up into the narrative machinery? "Mayhap it was this, the love that might have been, that lent to her softlyfeatured face at whiles a look, tense with suppressed meaning, that imparted a strange yearning tendency to the beautiful eyes a charm few could resist" [348/346].† Those are her words though she speaks no such sentence. Uncle Charles, puffing away at his pipe in the outhouse he calls "his arbour" is a Namer, and deserves to have something named after him. So let us designate the Uncle Charles Principle: *the narrative idiom need not be the narrator's*.

The Uncle Charles Principle may extend from diction to syntax. Syntax maps a set of judgments about relatedness, and such judgments help define the people who make them. So Joycean syntax may mirror the priorities of a character we needn't think of as framing the sentence. The conjunction at the hinge of a sentence about Gerty MacDowell's face—

The waxen pallor of her face was almost spiritual in its ivory-like purity though her rosebud mouth was a genuine Cupid's bow, Greekly perfect. [348/346]

—is neither an "and," assembling effects out of pallor and rosebud, nor a "but," disjoining their allegations (saint's complexion but sinner's lips); it is "though," and it wobbles like Gerty's half-formed notion that the ivory and the rose, the Spiritual and the Cupidinous, though conventionally incompatible may thanks after all to good taste—*this* sentence cannot be finished.

The next sentence of Joyce's text illustrates a different use for "though:"

Her hands were of finely veined alabaster with tapering fingers and as white as lemon juice and queen of ointments

†Page references to *Ulysses* appear as a double number in the form [425/429]. The first refers to what has become by default the international standard edition, the reset Random House of 1961; the second to the British Penguin edition of 1969.

could make them though it was not true that she used to wear kid gloves in bed or take a milk footbath either. [348/346]

This is a "though" to fend off malicious rumors, affirming, not without petulance (note the finely placed "either"), that much of her beauty is God-given. Later an "and" is eagerly affirmative, daring all, daring utter confusion even:

She had cut it that very morning on account of the new moon and it nestled about her pretty head in a profusion of luxuriant clusters and pared her nails too, Thursday for wealth. [349/347]

So eager is the second "and" to join "pared" with "cut"—Gerty has performed the due rituals, has observed the moon and the Thursday—that it crumples syntax (was it hair that pared?) in flushed impetuosity.

A *chef d'oeuvre* of expressive disarray is discoverable a few pages on, when Gerty meditates on the fortune that might have been hers (rolling in her carriage, second to none) had her father but avoided the clutches of the demon drink:

Over and over had she told herself that as she mused by the dying embers in a brown study without the lamp because she hated two lights or oftentimes gazing out of the window dreamily by the hour at the rain falling on the rusty bucket, thinking.[354/352]

Resolutely suppressing the suspicion that Gerty may think a brown study is a dun-colored Irish back room, we lend ear to that terminal cadence: "the rain falling . . . , thinking." The participles insist on chiming in parallel. Is it possible that "thinking" can go with "rain"? Does its sound mime the *tink tink* of rain in a bucket? Perhaps. More certainly, expressive in its valiant displacement, it closes the sentence where the sentence opened, not with rain and bucket but with Gerty deep in thought. And thought. And thought.

Though our spectrum of examples is incomplete even for "Nausicaa"—it omits for instance the shifting antecedents of Gerty's he's and him's, a prenominal promiscuity she shares with Molly Bloom—still it isn't misleadingly brief. Joyce's repertory of syntactic devices is not extensive. He is not, like Beckett, an Eiffel nor a Calder of the sentence. The single word— "repaired"; "salubrious"—is his normal means to his characteristic effects. His sentences, on the whole, suffice to get the words together, and when he is unsure of himself, in an early draft for instance or a bread-and-butter letter, entangled priorities will entangle his constructions as gracelessly as Gerty's though less entertainingly. The paragraph in *Stephen Hero* (Chapter XIX) in which Mr. Dedalus Sr. investigates Ibsen is as ill-written a draft as a major author has left; for instance,

A metaphor is a vice that attracts the dull mind by reason of its aptness and repels the too serious mind by reason of its falsity and danger so that, after all, there is something to be said, nothing voluminous perhaps, but at least a word of concession for that class of society which in literature as in everything else goes always with its four feet on the ground.

Dreiser was never worse. Joyce was simply unsure how much fun he wanted to poke at his father.

The letter to Bennet Cerf reprinted in the Random House *Ulysses* contains quite as much awkwardness:

This brave woman risked what professional publishers did not wish to, she took the manuscript and handed it to the printers. These were very scrupulous and understanding French printers in Dijon, the capital of the French printing press. In fact I attached no small importance to the work being done well and quickly. My eyesight still permitted me at that time to read the proofs myself and thus it came about that thanks to extra work and the kindness of Mr. Darantière the well-known Dijon printer *Ulysses* came out a very short time after the manuscript had been delivered and the first printed copy was sent to me for my fortieth birthday on the second of February 1922.

This seems cobbled together out of phrase-books by a fluent foreigner. "The capital of the French printing press" sounds like a misapprehended idiom. On the threshold of the third sentence we find "In fact" performing a wholly vacuous gesture, and the final sentence fumbles for its destination, buying time with "and" clauses and monstrosities such as "thus it came about that." We may learn from such mishaps that when Joyce was unsure of his role words swarmed in his head but all syntactic sense deserted him. Syntax was a function of role: of character.

Writing fiction, he played parts, and referred stylistic decisions to the taste of the person he was playing. The Uncle Charles Principle entails writing about someone much as that someone would choose to be written about. So it requires a knowledge of the character at which no one could arrive by "observation," and yet its application to the character seems as external as costume, since it does not entail recording spoken words. (We hear Gerty MacDowell speak just two short sentences.)

Part of Joyce's preparation for writing "Nausicaa" (October–February 1919–20) was his period of moony absorption with Martha Fleischmann (December–

February 1918–19). Obsessing himself with what she must be thinking of his overtures, he was learning to play both sides of a voyeurist episode. His preparation for undertaking *Ulysses* included learning to play a middle-aged Jew. This was the most ambitious thing he undertook in his life, since it entailed presenting in intimate detail a character of whose world he had no real knowledge, and it was more than a year after work was begun on the book that he could announce the completion of even one episode.

He needed to make up his mind who his hero was. Bloom needed a name, an age, a birthplace; needed a family history as far back at least as he would be even dimly aware of it, which meant back to his grandfather's generation; needed experiences, tastes, opinions; needed mannerisms and habits, mental and physical; and needed to have defined on his behalf his relationship to the Jewish heritage he never fully assumed and has tried to relinquish though he cannot forget it. All this received plausible working-out with the help of Joyce's Triestine Jewish friends: a considerable feat for a writer who had always worked with lower-class Irish Catholic milieux he knew intimately, and with characters who were either modelled on himself or else were so like himself that with different luck he might have become them.

Yet Bloom is not a "case" worked up: the Jew in Dublin. That is because Joyce built him, as he did all characters, by playing him. He found the role congenial. Though Dublin Jewry seems not to have been part of his Dublin experience, he could project important aspects of Bloom out of his own sense of having been always odd man out, excluded by disinclination, weak sight and independent intellect from the boisterous milieu his father had meant him to enter, excluded by poverty, by Catholicism and by unclubbability from the Anglo-Irish milieu in which Yeats cut so distinguished a figure. And Bloom holds very much the opinions of James Joyce on a wide range of Dublin topics: on Irish nationalism, on drunkenness, on literary pretensions, on death and resurrection, on marriage, on the hierarchy of the virtues.

Wyndham Lewis, again the most helpful of devil's advocates, saw in Bloom simply the author disguised as a stage Jew, and there is enough truth in this remark to point up what at an early stage of the enterprise Joyce would have seen as his principal technical difficulty: to prevent Bloom from becoming yet one more version of himself, differing from other "Joyce characters" in no more than accessory matters, stature, coloring, age, and racial heritage.

The danger was the greater because Joyce had determined to present Bloom largely from the inside. Fiction's individuating detail has traditionally been external, an affair of quirks and mannerisms which belong to the self presented to an observer, and vanish once we plunge beneath surface behavior. How very alike are the half-conscious minds presented by Mrs. Woolf or Dorothy Richardson!—one semi-transparent envelope much like another, "stream of consciousness" an undifferentiating verbal soup.

The extreme of externality, though, is the stage, and in the months before writing the first sentence of *Ulysses* Joyce as though by precaution also wrote a three-act play. There are canonical things to be said about the play, as that he needed to get Ibsen out of his system, or that he needed to treat the theme of infidelity in a way that would discharge his own feelings and suspicions, so he could handle it calmly in the novel. Such discussion is apt to protract itself by way of evading what the critic feels is his real, unwelcome, duty: to state that *Exiles* is not much of a play. It is not; and they aim a quip accurately in Dublin when they claim—many jokesters claim it—to be working on "a dramatization of *Exiles*." Still "the man of genius makes no mistakes," and Joyce, with the new novel growing in his mind, was right to devote some months to the composition of *Exiles*.

He needed to write something with no point of view, no narrator, whatever: something wholly "objective": something in which the only point of view would be that of the spectator, making what can be made of the characters when nothing is accessible but their speeches and their behavior. What happens when the storyteller gets as far outside his story as that?

When the writer is Joyce, what happens is that he loses control; the characters do not reveal themselves sufficiently. Joyce has persuaded us, with the aid of Stephen Dedalus, that he occupied a position of quasi-invisibility, "refined out of existence, indifferent, paring his fingernails." But that, by Stephen's own analysis, is the dramatist's position, and neither *Dubliners* nor *Ulysses* is drama. The point of view, in these fictions, is somewhere within the fiction. We see, for instance, over Eveline's shoulder, and misread severely if we fail to notice this fact. It is only plays that have no point of view within them. What looks like narrative is instructions for actors; what looks like description is instructions for the set-dresser.

For the second act of *Exiles* the set-dresser is instructed to equip "a room in Robert Hand's cottage" with a piano, a large table, upholstered chairs near this table, a small cardtable, a bookcase, a sideboard, a standing Turkish pipe, a low oil stove, a rocking chair, also "assorted chairs here and there." The stage at the old Abbey could never have absorbed all that. It is a crowded room we are to envisage, comically jammed with the appurtenances of a 1912 bachelor's bower of bliss. The actor playing Robert Hand next gets his instructions. He is to sit at the piano and play "softly in the bass" a specified air from *Tannhäuser*. Then he must rest an elbow on the edge of the keyboard and meditate. After that "he rises, and pulling out a pump from behind the piano, walks here and there in the room ejecting from it into the air sprays of perfume. He inhales the air slowly and puts the pump back behind the piano." (Pause here to imagine the expression the actor must take care to assume as he "inhales the air slowly.") There is more. "He sits down on a chair near the table, and, smoothing his hair carefully, sighs once or twice. Then, thrusting his hands into his trousers pockets, he leans back, stretches out his legs, and waits." If by this time the audience is not helpless with laughter it may hear a knock, and his cry as he rises, "Bertha!" And it is not Bertha but Bertha's husband who enters.

This is capital farce, and so is some of the first-act dialogue:

RICHARD: You plighted your troth, as they say, with a kiss. And you gave him your garter. Is it allowed to mention that?

BEATRICE, *with some reserve:* If you think it worthy of mention.

Unhappily *Exiles* refuses to be a farce; it wants to be a strenuous drama of ideals. Drama is more ritualistic than Joyce appears to have supposed. If it is not to enact straightforwardly the ritual of farce or the ritual of pathos, then its recourse must be, as Shakespeare knew, to the ritual of a formal language which can hold the farcical and the tragic in suspension. "By the discandying of this pelleted storm," says Cleopatra, anticipating in her *O Altitudo*! embalmization in a syrup of hail. But Joyce wanted his actors to exchange sentences of plain decent prose.

So in *Exiles* he tried out what he could do with a medium in which the spectators merely look and listen. Less than needed doing, it seemed; and though he would affirm to the last his faith in that play he never tried anything at all like it again. It remained an extreme toward which he could gauge his approximations, and in the great novel, when he seems to be *showing* us like a playwright, he can judge just which little nudges and inflections, of a kind unavailable to the playwright, will be necessary to make his effect secure. Here, to contrast with Robert Hand and his perfume-pump, is a glimpse of another bachelor-seducer:

The blond girl in Thornton's bedded the wicker basket with rustling fibre. Blazes Boylan handed her the bottle swathed in pink tissue paper and a small jar.

—Put these in first, will you? he said.

—Yes sir, the blond girl said, and the fruit on top.

—That'll do, game ball, Blazes Boylan said.

She bestowed fat pears neatly, head by tail, and among them ripe shamefaced peaches.

Blazes Boylan walked here and there in new tan shoes about the fruitsmelling shop, lifting fruits, young juicy crinkled and plump red tomatoes, sniffing smells. [227/226]

He is buying what he conceives will be a trigger for Molly Bloom's sensuality, and arranging to have it arrive at 7 Eccles Street shortly before he does. The strategem is transparent, and the presentation seems impersonal throughout. Yet little touches ensure it: Boylan-verbs: "The blond girl *bedded* the wicker basket"; Boylan-epithets: "She bestowed *fat* pears neatly, head by tail, and among them *ripe shamefaced* peaches." And the fruits Boylan lifts are young and juicy and plump and red. Many hours later when Bloom returns to his kitchen he will eye amid the clutter of its cupboard "an oval wicker basket bedded with fibre and containing one Jersey pear," and "a halfempty bottle of William Gilbey and Co's white invalid port, half disrobed of its swathe of coralpink tissue paper" [675/595]. There is "bedded" again, and there, in proximity with another of Boylan's lures, is another Boylan-word, "disrobed." It is with such tiny nudges that we are taught the right reading of the signatures of all things.

So *Ulysses* is comfortable with its comic dimension as *Exiles* is not. Constantly prompting us by an intricate notation of diction and rhythm, it frees us even to smile in the course of a funeral. A narrative passage opens:

The priest took a stick with a knob at the end of it out of the boy's bucket and shook it over the coffin. Then he walked to the other end and shook it again. Then he came back and put it back in the bucket. As you were before you rested. It's all written down: he has to do it. [104/105–106]

This is the report of the innocent eye, and the comment ("He has to do it") is from Bloom. It is as though

Gulliver were describing an Irish funeral to the Houyhnhnms. And next we hear a solemn liturgical cadence, always for Joyce a positive value:

> —*Et ne nos inducas in tentationem.*
> The server piped the answers in the treble. I often thought it would be better to have boy servants. Up to fifteen or so. After that of course . . . [104/106]

—Which is Bloom responding not to the cadence but to the fact that it comes in a boy's voice, and checking himself from a too rash abandonment of female scullerymaids (he hasn't understood the prayer not to be led into temptation). Then he thinks back to the stick with the knob at the end of it:

> Holy water that was I expect. Shaking sleep out of it. He must be fed up with that job, shaking that thing over all the corpses they trot up. [104/106]

(How like Bloom, to feel compassion for a bored worker!)

> What harm if he could see what he was shaking it over. Every mortal day a fresh batch: middleaged men, old women, children, women dead in childbirth, men with beards, baldheaded business men, consumptive girls with little sparrow's breasts. All the year round he prayed the same thing over them all and shook water on top of them: sleep. On Dignam now. [104/106]

Here something has subtly happened. What commenced as Bloom's list of mortuary variousness has insensibly become the narrator's: "consumptive girls with little sparrow's breasts" seems too shapely in its cadence to have sprung from Bloom's mind. And sure enough, the tense has shifted from the monologue present to the narrative past: "All year round he prayed the same thing over them all." . . . And: "Sleep. On Dignam now." Then Latin once more, adroitly apt:

—*In Paradisum.*
Said he was going to paradise or is in paradise. Says that over everybody. Tiresome kind of a job. But he has to say something. [104/106]

We are back with the comedy of Bloom's *maladresse*, having touched on pathos perhaps without quite knowing how. For an unobtrusive moment superior skills took over, to supply "young girls with little sparrow's breasts" and the solemn "On Dignam now" and *"In paradisum."* And checking itself, this movement on reverting to irreverence is protected by our knowledge that Bloom is present, since what would be cynical coming from the author is commonsensical coming from Bloom. So Bloom and the narrator cooperate in rapidly flickering effects.

The description of the Holy Water being sprinkled gains its grotesque effect from Bloom's innocence. Again it would be auctorial cynicism, this writing of sticks and buckets from a pen that is ready when it chooses with the proper Latin term for anything. If we want a precedent for its comedy we need go no further than Lilliput, where the inventory of what is in Gulliver's pockets relies in a similar way on the Lilliputians' inexperience with what they are describing. They do their best to verbalize what is presented to them, for instance "a Globe, half Silver, and half of some transparent Metal: For in the transparent Side we saw certain strange Figures circularly drawn, and thought we could touch them, until we found our Fingers stopped with that lucid Substance. He put this

Engine to our Ears, which made an incessant Noise
like that of a Water-Mill." This Engine of course is
Gulliver's watch. There is always a lack of economy in
not knowing the name of something, and being driven
to descriptive periphrasis, which ministers to the
comic. It is like the sentence about Robert Hand in
Exiles, after the business with the perfume-pump,
when "He sits down on a chair near the table, and
smoothing his hair carefully, sighs once or twice":
oddly funnier in the description than it would be in the
performance, because the description is external to the
action as the Lilliputians were external to a knowledge
of Gulliver's watch, whereas we assume that an actor
knows what passion he is portraying, and wait to see
what it may be.

Description without knowledge is always potentially comic. It fails of intimacy with what is described.
Being outside, it enacts a certain bafflement, as though
it were a periphrasis for the intimate identifying word,
such as Watch. That is one reason Joyce drives himself,
in *Ulysses,* to many little triumphs of linguistic virtuosity. He needs, in the ordinary texture of his narrative, to convey the illusion that things are being named
exactly; then Bloom's monologue, draped over the
surface of things, will have the comic texture of periphrasis. So when the funeral coach arrives at Glas-
nevin we meet an unobtrusive neologism: "The felly
harshed against the curbstone: stopped" [100/102].
"Felly" is technical, "harshed" is novel; the reader is
unlikely to be specially conscious of either; such constructions, in this book, are parts of the normal narrative machinery. They serve to set off such Bloomish
ramblings as:

Coffin now. Got here before us, dead as he is. Horse looking round at us with his plume skeowways. Dull eye: collar tight on his neck, pressing on a bloodvessel or something. Do they know what they cart out here every day? [101/103]

—once more the comic outsider, with his speculations on the thoughts and feelings of an undertaker's drafthorse. Bloom's mind beats its wings against fact like a moth against a lamp: not for him the narrator's effortless symbiosis of phenomenon with word.

Joyce's minor virtuosities are so deft, so frequent, so normally confined to one exact word or two, that we may quite fail to notice his reversal of the normal practice of fiction: it is in the little bits of narrator's machinery, introducing speeches, specifying places, getting things and characters from place to place, that the language is apt to be especially inventive, and it is the words of Bloom that are apt to be flat and ordinary. The odd effect is that Bloom seems a great comic creation, his locutions crisp and bright and unpredictable. This convention is established in our first moments with Bloom:

Another slice of bread and butter: three, four: right. She didn't like her plate full. Right. He turned from the tray, lifted the kettle off the hob and set it sideways on the fire. It sat there, dull and squat, its spout stuck out. Cup of tea soon. Good. Mouth dry. The cat walked stiffly round a leg of the table with tail on high.
—Mkgnao!
—O, there you are, Mr Bloom said, turning from the fire. [55/57]

It is the narrative machinery that makes the kettle "dull

and squat," and has the cat walk "with tail on high" and utter that exotic sound where we should expect a standard "Meow." Language like "O, there you are" and "Another slice of bread and butter" comes from Bloom. So Bloom's consciousness hovers outside the varied phenomena which we find the narrator commanding with such intimacy of nomenclature, like the one man in Lilliput who should know enough to say "Watch."

By this very simple device Joyce outflanked the problem we stated a few pages back, the problem of keeping Bloom's monologue separated from his own narrative, and hence from his own judgments. This was a delicate business in the funeral episode, where we surmise that his and Bloom's evaluation of the worth of what was going on tended to coincide, though with this difference, that he knew as Bloom did not what the rituals and the Latin meant. Yet his purpose in exploiting Bloom's ignorance was not to make a fool of Bloom, nor even to provoke the kind of smiles the Lilliputians bestir in knowing readers as they struggle with that massive ticking engine. The only value he chooses to extract from the liturgical Latin is rhythmic and sonorous, and as for the besprinkling of the coffin, he forces us to see what is after all happening. A contrast of textures emerges, not a contrast of knowledges.

From this often subliminal contrast between the careful recital of events, or the careful description of surfaces, and the swift knowing intimate Name, an odd conclusion emerges: that the domain of the interior monologue is actually external. It is the idiom of the perpetual outsider. "Be a warm day I fancy. Specially in these black clothes feel it more. Black conducts, reflects (refracts is it?) the heat" [57/59]. Bloom is outside his theme, fumbling for its knob; the word he can't think of is "absorbs." Something similar happens amid his lyrical fantasies: "Fading gold sky. A mother watches from her doorway. She calls her children home in their dark language. High wall: beyond strings twanged. Night sky moon, violet, colour of Molly's new garters. Strings. Listen. A girl playing one of those instruments what do you call them: dulcimers. I pass" [57/59]. The author has lent some unobtrusive help with the shaping of such a phrase as "their dark language," but the adduction of Molly's new garters and the "what do you call them" dulcimers is pure Bloom, never at home with the idiom even of reverie, not even with James Joyce to lend a hand.

Joyce plays two roles then, Bloom and the narrator. The narrator, who can put most things accurately in a word or two (cheerfully defying as he does so most normal canons of diction) affords an unobtrusive paradigm against which we gauge the resistance the same things present to Bloom's mind. Here the book appeals to a subliminal sense of ours, more powerful than our regard for canons of diction: that economy ought to be attainable, that somewhere, for everything that wants expressing, a single apt word exists like a name bestowed by Adam. Alongside that hinted norm Bloom seems periphrastic, traversing as he does an inordinate number of words. Even his most telegraphic thoughts, those chains of sentence-fragments, are periphrastic. In its very economy his monologue is verbose.

We may now notice something about the pace of the book, a consequence of the frequently noticed fact that its episodes tend to grow longer and longer. As they grow longer Bloom has less and less to say; the periphrases no longer emanate from him, but from the narrative mind. Accordingly Bloom, without really changing his manner, seems to become a man of fewer and fewer words, and after a while his most inept remarks have by contrast with their surroundings the concision of lapidary wisdom. Hence such complex effects as the one in the Cyclops' tavern, where Bloom is accused of boring everyone to death with endless talk which is barely audible thanks to the narrator's endless talk, and where perhaps his most fatuous remark of the day seems like a pearl of wisdom: "Love, says Bloom. I mean the opposite of hatred" [333/331]. The anonymous narrator of this episode is responsible for half a hundred pages of vigorous idiosyncratic language, appallingly energized contempt; he is the epitomized Irish tavern talker, fine flower of what book-people have learned to envy as an oral culture; and it is Bloom's definition of love that is the most memorable thing that gets said.

So we now have one clue to the stylistic elaborations in the latter half of the book: they reverse the principle of the early Bloom chapters—Bloom fumbling and garrulous, the narrative concise and economical. By "Cyclops"—somewhat before the half-way mark—it is in Bloom's direction, not in the narrator's, that we look for economy. Joyce told Frank Budgen that he meant Bloom to grow in stature throughout the day, and indeed amid the stylistic caprice of the later episodes he sounds as pithy as a pre-Socratic philosopher.

Having committed himself to doing everything wrong the better to make Bloom look right, Joyce had assumed the uniquely intricate burden of making the multifold wrongness also seem right, right enough for the book in its extravagances to cohere. This brings us back to the Uncle Charles Principle, which despite appearances is not abandoned. The Uncle Charles Principle, we remember, entails applying the character's sort of wording to the character. In one of the late episodes of *Ulysses* we find Bloom written about as he would choose. The result is a contrived stylistic disaster.

Still, Bloom deserved the courtesy of the experiment. It comes at his finest moment, at the one time in his long day when, snubbed, thwarted, cuckolded, ignored, jeered at, slandered, put upon, he is finally entitled to feel like a hero. For he has taken initiative after initiative, has stood up to a drunken soldier, has contrived the deliverance of Stephen Dedalus from multiple enemies, has assumed responsibility for his safety, and is now about to go home with a genuine Poet-Philosopher in tow. At last he feels like the hero of a novel, which for Joyce in fiction after fiction is the apotheosis to which fictional beings aspire. And he has his reward. He is treated to an episode written as he would have written it. The language is solemn, decorated, fulsome, periphrastic. The episode is the one called "Eumaeus."

It commences "Preparatory to anything else," a Bloomish trumpet-flourish of a beginning.

Preparatory to anything else Mr Bloom brushed off the greater bulk of the shavings and handed Stephen the hat and ashplant and bucked him up generally in orthodox Samaritan fashion, which he very badly needed. [612–13/533]

There, as the book's third part opens, are "brush" and "shaving" and "Buck," three words that on the very first page of the book served to define a wholly different scene. Brushing aside (so to speak) a hallucinatory Mulligan with a shaving-brush, we query "orthodox Samaritan fashion." There's English for you! But may one put "orthodox" beside "Samaritan"? No, one had better not, because "orthodox" conjures up "Jew," which is antithetic to "Samaritan." But the word "Jew" is not here? Ah, but (quite apart from the race of Mr. Bloom's father) the word "Samaritan" helps bring it here. So words do battle with the ghosts of absent words.

Next we learn of the hope that they "might hit upon some drinkables in the shape of a milk and soda or a mineral" [613/533], and there rises within each reader a ghostly schoolmaster to protest that drinkables are not for hitting, and liquids proverbially have no shape; moreover by what appeal to absent idiom does "a mineral" become the shape of a drinkable?

Soon a cab is sighted, and we observe "Mr Bloom, who was anything but a professional whistler" endeavoring "to hail it by emitting a kind of a whistle" [613/533]. Penumbrally these words conjure up some "professional whistler" (to be distinguished from an amateur whistler), and "a kind of a whistle" which presumably is not a mainstream whistle.

Wonder crowds upon wonder. In a "quandary" (a word Bloom would enjoy using) the two next "put a good face on the matter and foot it" [613/533–34] (how pliable is the anatomy of "the matter"!). Immediately thereafter Mr. Bloom, patient Laocoon, is said to be "handicapped" by a "circumstance," which if we are to credit etymology stands around him hand in cap, before it is suddenly equated with the absence of a button. But he enters "thoroughly into the spirit of the thing" [613–14/534] (as we fumble round for that in-

spirited "thing") and "heroically" (being after all
Ulysses) "makes light" of the mischance (*Fiat lux*).
Next they "dandered along past by where the empty
vehicle was waiting without a fare or a jarvey" [614/
534]; we do not know whether to marvel more at the
reduplicated emptiness or at the concatenated "along
past by where," a procession of phantom constructions.

It is in "Eumaeus," more than anywhere else in
Ulysses that we find the principles of *Finnegans Wake* on
display, congesting foreground and middle distance
with verbal phantoms. And if we open *Finnegans Wake*
at random it is "Eumaeus"-like syntax that we are apt
to find. No episode in Ulysses would pose more in-
superable obstacles for a translator. "Dandered along
past by where . . ."!—what might a committee of
Frenchmen hope to do with that?

And it is so much Bloom's episode he even day-
dreams of writing it: "Suppose he were to pen something out of the common groove (as he fully intended
doing) at the rate of one guinea per column, *My Experiences*, let us say, *in a Cabman's Shelter*" [647/567]. He
would write it, we may feel sure, the way it is written,
obeying a principle T. S. Eliot discerned in the diction
of Byron:

Just as an artisan who can talk English beautifully while
about his work or in a public bar, may compose a letter
painfully written in a dead language bearing some resemblance to a newspaper leader, and decorated with words
like "maelstrom" and "pandemonium": so does Byron
write a dead or dying language.

When Bloom is represented as speaking in this
episode—and only in this episode—what he says is apt

to be continuous with its narrative texture; he says, "Analogous scenes are occasionally, if not often, met with" [636/556] and "It has been explained by competent men as the convolutions of the grey matter" [633/554]. Everyone else talks realistically; Stephen says things like "All too Irish" [623/543] and "Count me out" [644/565]; the garrulous sailor says "There was lice in that bunk in Bridgwater sure as nuts" [631/551]. Only Bloom uses polysyllables: as though for these fifty pages he held the pen, and could reserve the most stylish lines for himself.

"Eumaeus" has been called cliché-ridden, therefore tired. Tired it is not. There is no one—no, not at Harvard—who could write three consecutive sentences of it, fatigued or alert. It is open to wonder whether any episode cost Joyce such pains, plumbing depths of expressive infelicity most of us have not the talent even to conceive. And we are meant to suppose that Bloom might be executing it, had he the time and the freedom from distraction. Copious in its fecund awfulness, it is Joyce's return to the tonic of his method: the Uncle Charles Principle *in excelsis*, a stylistic homage in Bloom's style to Bloom, and in some ways the book's most profound tribute to its hero, Ulysses, first among Homer's word-men.

3. Myth and Pyrrhonism

There were few things that could hold James Joyce's attention like the spectacle of a man speaking in public. The preacher, the barrister, the after-dinner speaker, performs a paradigmatic communal act, offering to make sense, coherent sense, of what he and his listeners confront together. So, toward the end of that bewildering dinner-party "in the dark, gaunt house on Usher's Island," we find Gabriel Conroy leaning his ten trembling fingers on the tablecloth and smiling nervously before he utters the ritual words "Ladies and Gentlemen" and staggers from cliché to cliché into exegetical disaster. It is his private belief that his aunts are ignorant old women and that he is orating to vulgarians. Accordingly he is shamelessly formulaic. He says "my poor powers," he says "take the will for the deed," he even says "last but not least." Soaring higher, he offers to explicate the evening by myth, the way Joyce later taught us to perform an explication. He identifies his aunts and their niece as the Three Graces of the Dublin Musical World. (What did he say? asks Aunt Julia. "'He says we are the Three Graces, Aunt Julia,' said Mary Jane.") He then entangles himself in a wholly unnoticed confusion between the Three Graces and the three goddesses in the story of the Judgment of Paris, and leads the company in song while "Freddy Malins beat time with his pudding-fork." It is what we have learned to identify as a thoroughly Joycean occasion.

Gabriel has offered us two myths, jumbled together. Not even unjumbled would either one really fit. But by the end of the story there is a myth that fits, though it does not belong to the story's public occasion, and Gabriel had no reason to think of it. This is the myth of Orpheus. He has played Orpheus, and failed as Orpheus failed. He has sought to lead Gretta up from the land of The Dead, up to where moments of their life together were "like the tender fire of stars," but has made the Orphic mistake of looking back ("I suppose you were in love with this Michael Furey, Gretta"). So she sleeps, communing with the dead, and he gazes through the cold window at the snow.

That is how it is apt to be in the Joyce Country. People posture, people play roles, people fit themselves into myths, even venture explications. But the myths of which they are conscious are not the right ones, nor the explications either coherent or applicable. They are part of the apparatus of foreground posture, blending readily with available cliché. Cliché is wonderfully accommodating: instant myth. Eveline sitting at the window plays, more or less unconsciously, a pre–Raphaelite maiden. Mrs. Mooney rehearses, quite deliberately, the part of Outraged Mother. Stephen Dedalus plays the dissolute bard, and also Hamlet ("my Hamlet hat" [47/53], he remarks in self-appreciation). Leopold Bloom plays, not willingly, the cuckold of classic farce, and toys with playing Mozart's Stone Guest, nemesis of the facile Don. Stephen does not know he is Telemachus, and Bloom does not know he is Ulysses. Only we (prompted by a book's title) know such things: that their postures are the wavering reproductions of great archetypal postures: that they unwittingly mock a heroic which mocks them.

In *Dubliners* Joyce had kept his language on the whole transparent, a medium through which we perceive the goings-on which we are to comprehend as the characters do not. *Ulysses,* it is well known, was first conceived as another story in the *Dubliners* manner, and when Joyce began to write it as a novel he set about the job in a relatively straightforward way, employing as always the Uncle Charles Principle and also his chief new device, the Interior Monologue, but on the whole—a restriction we shall look at later— keeping close enough to Objectivity not to frighten a reader who had mastered *A Portrait of the Artist as a Young Man.*

But with the eleventh episode, called "Sirens," something changed, and so radically that the author's staunchest advocate, Ezra Pound, was dismayed.★ (Would these events really lose, Pound wrote to ask, by being told in "simple Maupassant"?) For no longer do we see the foreground postures directly, in order to see past them perhaps to Homer. Our immediate awareness now is of screens of language, through or past which it is not easy to see.

The language is what we now confront, as in *Dubliners* we had confronted the characters. A list of some fifty-eight linguistic fragments opens the episode. A thematic index? The skeleton of an overture? Not a narrative continuity anyhow. And as the episode develops the language is doing very much what the characters had previously done: playing roles, striking postures, contorting itself into expressive patterns which offer to clarify what is going on and instead, like

Gabriel Conroy's speech, mislead: introducing disso-
nance into the ancient doctrine of stylistic decorum.
"Sirens," "Cyclops," "Nausicaa," above all "Oxen of
the Sun": in these four consecutive episodes what may
plausibly be described as a brilliant adaptation of
means to ends becomes on further scrutiny simply,
elaborately wrong, an aspect, so to speak, of Dublin's
wonderful readiness with misinterpretation. Like the
judgments various Dubliners render on Leopold
Bloom—as that the Freemasons are looking after him,
or that he has made a killing on the Gold Cup—these
contortions of language pervert the silent human reality, and we may come to think them perverse.

Bloom's human reality is especially silent in "Sirens," as he waits out the book's first climax: the
dreaded hour when Blazes Boylan and Molly are to
sing in the parlor and tumble in the bed at 7 Eccles
Street. Toward this event seven consecutive episodes
have pointed: it is the consummation of Bloom's role
as cuckold, of Molly's role as amateur of adultery. Like
most "big" scenes in Joyce, like the outrages in Greek
tragedy, it happens offstage. We may usefully compare
its handling in *Ulysses* with another of Joyce's offstage
climaxes, the confrontation of Bob Doran by Mrs.
Mooney in "The Boarding House."

Mrs. Mooney's scene we have no difficulty in vis-
ualizing. She will see to its structure, we know; and we
have heard her running over the heads of her speech:
"outraged mother"; "abused her hospitality"; "simply taken advantage of Polly's youth and inexperience"; "loss of her daughter's honour." Like all sum-
mary speeches delivered by Joyce characters, like
Gabriel Conroy's dinner oration for instance, this
eloquence of hers is inaccurate to the point of grotes-

querie. Of course accuracy is not the point; the point is that the oration will work. Bob Doran will propose marriage.

While this climactic oration is being delivered, the reader of "The Boarding House" is detained with Polly. Polly's mind is elsewhere, insofar as it can be said to be anywhere. She entertains "secret, amiable memories," and falls into "a reverie." She is neither here, in her bedroom, nor there, where the great confrontation is in progress. Nevertheless we readers are in no perplexity. We know, while we wait with Polly and while her memories gradually give place to "hopes and visions of the future," we know exactly what is going on downstairs. And when we hear Mrs. Mooney's uplifted voice, "Come down, dear. Mr Doran wants to speak to you," we are quite sure what he will say, and quite sure why.

But now contrast the hour of assignation in *Ulysses*. Nothing at all is that clear. There is even some slight doubt whether Boylan will after all keep the rendezvous ("At four. Has he forgotten? Perhaps a trick. Not come: whet appetite" [266/265].) And though we wait with Bloom as in a different book we waited with Polly, we are offered nothing as definite as the crisp prose in which Polly "rested the nape of her neck against the cool iron bedstead and fell into a reverie." No, in the foreground a stylistic caper is in process, intricately inappropriate; nothing less, if we are to trust the schema,★ than an effort to construct a prose *fuga per canonem*: as though, to amuse us while Agamemnon dies, a magician were to attempt the levitation of Cassandra, absorbing the full attention of the Chorus.

Literal music is woven into this fugue, none of it tactfully chosen. The piano is played: the unvoiced

words are "Goodbye, Sweetheart, Goodbye" [267/
266]. Ben Dollard sings "When Love Absorbs my Ar-
dent Soul" [270/268], electing by mistake the words
for the tenor part though his voice is bass baritone.
Richie Goulding whistles "All is lost now" [272/271],
from an opera about a maiden who sleepwalked into
trouble, and we may disentangle from the intricacies of
the page Bloom's effort to apply this paradigm: "In
sleep she went to him. Innocence in the moon. Still
hold her back. Brave, don't know their danger. Call
name. Touch water. Jingle jaunty. Too late. She
longed to go. That's why. Woman. As easy as the sea.
Yes: all is lost" [272–73/271]. It is not the right
paradigm, since Molly has not been in a trance of any
description. Si Dedalus sings "Co-me, thou lost one"
[275/274] from the opera *Martha*, and we are told how

Through the hush of air a voice sang to them, low, not rain,
not leaves in murmur, like no voice of strings of reeds or
whatdoyoucallthem dulcimers, touching their still ears with
words, still hearts of their each his remembered lives. [273–
74/272]

We may pause on this sentence: it illustrates admirably the intricate indecorums of "Sirens." In its zest for
the mimetic it partly obscures the syntax of what it is
saying ("still hearts of their each his remembered
lives"). What it is saying in turn misleads, since "low,
not rain, not leaves in murmur, like no voice of strings
of reeds" makes a ritual of excluding options unlikely
to be entertained. It solicits awe of its own intricate
mimesis, which it compromises by the stumbled
"whatdoyoucallthem," a Bloom-word from an earlier
encounter of his mind with dulcimers, though surely

we are not to suppose that the sentence we are reading passes through Bloom's consciousness. What is never far from Bloom's consciousness is the front hall at 7 Eccles Street, where he imagines, torments himself by imagining,

Knock. Last look at the mirror always before she answers the door. The hall. There? How do you do? I do well. There? What? Or? [274/273]

And he is willing to listen to the singing, which both distracts him from these sad events and solicits him with their lyricism. It is a pathetic and poignant tableau. And all this while a glittering kaleidoscope of words is letting us know what is supposed to be really important: a performance that sacrifices all pathos and poignancy to sounding dross and tinkling syllable.

This principle, which grows more marked as *Ulysses* proceeds, exploits a certain impertinence of language to event, extending the principle that Dublin's own summaries, for instance Gabriel's after-dinner speech, are pieces of inappropriate virtuosity. So is the poem about the "uncrowned king" at the end of "Ivy Day," which ends with a wince for the Parnellites by accenting the name Par*nell* though the elect say *Par*nell; so is the sermon at the end of "Grace"; so is Maria's song at the end of "Clay," which she gets wrong though no one will tell her; and so, we are saying, is the linguistic decorum of two-thirds of *Ulysses,* which insists on concealing the events and tensions we imagine are being clarified. A vast stylistic mistake, heavily ingenious, like the bust of Sir Philip Crampton about which Stephen Dedalus once asked an esthetic question (the placid head seemed to burst

MEMORIAL FOUNTAIN AT DUBLIN TO THE LATE SIR PHILIP
CRAMPTON, SURGEON-GENERAL OF HER MAJESTY'S FORCES.

The Crampton Memorial

from a bronze artichoke; was it lyrical, epical, or dramatic?)—such was the world Joyce was at pains to epitomize.

It is a world that makes a cult of nostalgia but is wholly devoid of any historical sense. ("Who was he?" [92/93] Bloom asks of Crampton: a candid question.) Who the great dead were, what it might have felt like to live in their world, as their contemporaries, Dublin does not care to wonder. All that matters is the polemical use of invoking them now, as Mrs. Mooney invokes the archetype of the wronged mother. It seems not to matter if the facts are wrong, like most of the facts which Joyce's people exchange about the Phoenix Park Murders or about Parnell.

And Joyce's own lack of any feel for the past—for any past more remote than the world his father could talk about—is one of the most striking aspects of his talent. Though abundant in historical and mythological paradigms, *Ulysses* tends to refuse us the sensations of time-travel. We are always in 1904. The contrast with the other great modernists is striking: with Pound's ability to step across some narrow threshold into vanished times—

> Set keel to breaker, forth on the godly sea, and
> We set up mast and sail on that swart ship,
> Bore sheep aboard her and our bodies also

—or Eliot's sudden dissolvings of London into mythological space:

> A crowd flowed over London Bridge, so many
> I had not thought death had undone so many.
> Sighs, short and infrequent, were exhaled,
> And each man fixed his eyes before his feet.
> Flowed up the hill and down King William Street . . .

For three lines London dissolves—there is no other word—and the moving crowd flows through some featureless domain where symbols throng: so intense in its identity, this domain, that King William Street, back in London, comes as a shock.

Joyce has no effects like this. The one deliberate time-journey in *Ulysses*, Stephen's evocation of the London of Shakespeare, detains our attention in the Dublin library where the words are spoken, and undercuts the words with swift remarks on how the trick is worked:

It is this hour of a day in mid-June, Stephen said, begging with a swift glance their hearing. The flag is up on the playhouse by the bankside. The bear Sackerson growls in the pit near it. Paris garden. Canvasclimbers who sailed with Drake chew their sausages among the groundlings.

Local colour. Work in all you know. Make them accomplices. [188/188]

No whatdoyoucallthem dulcimers could deflate an evocation more surely. All is words, we are being reminded, and all words are now.

That is why, in "The Oxen of the Sun," the effect of the successive prose parodies is so disorienting. Our persistent response to them is like our response to the intricate music of the Sirens, that they get in the way of our finding out what is happening. They produce this effect because we are deprived of the effect they might otherwise produce, the evocation of other times. This is not to complain that Joyce has not Pound's knack for pastiche, but to assert that he did not envy such a knack. We can even see him working against the grain of his parodies,★ to interfere with any propensity they may have for becoming evocative: one favorite device is to destroy the cadence of a sentence, so that it sings no tune and is uncertain of its own tempo and becomes an agglomeration of archaic words. Again, all is words, words. All the book, the book has been insisting, is words, arranged, rearranged.

In so atomizing his presentation, disjoining matter and manner, forcing against us a sheer stylistic arbitrariness, Joyce is refusing the most pervasive idea of the century in which he was born, the idea of continuity. In continuity, ran Romantic doctrine, lay health; thus by turning away from an imposed inheritance, the Graeco-Roman, toward an indigenous one—Anglo-Saxon, ballads—speech could recover sinewy authenticities. Darwin made continuity in time the theme of biology; etymologists made it the theme of linguistics. That great collective labor the *O.E.D.*, which is the English epic of the nineteenth century as Gibbon's *Decline and Fall* is the epic of the eighteenth and *Paradise Lost* the epic of the seventeenth, presents every usage current today as but our date's cross-section through an organic process extending back seamless to Indo-European. Such studies epitomize what Saussure has taught us to call the preoccupations of the diachronic, elements arrayed in time and our time a thin slice. It is easy to call Joyce the supreme artificer of Saussure's counterprinciple, the synchronic: all that exists exists only now, and the past is real only as I imagine it. "Synchronic" is a little too easy to say. We need to know how that alignment came about.

It came about in part because the sheer otherness of the past was a Romantic invention, and Romanticism skipped Ireland. Unless the past is other, your relationship can never be one of continuity, nor yet of discontinuity: only identity, with the costumes altered. So

Stephen has Shakespeare trudging to London whis-
tling *The girl I left behind me* [191/191], and asserts that
"his pageants, the histories, sail fullbellied on a tide
of Mafeking enthusiasm" [205/205]: the Armada an
episode in a seventeenth-century Boer War. Joyce in
the same way told Frank Budgen that Ulysses invented the tank: wooden horse or steel juggernaut, it
didn't matter. If Shakespeare's time seems other, or the
time of Ulysses, it is because we are deceived by costume, and if their speech sounds other, it is because we
are seduced by the surfaces of language, which is but
another kind of costume. Such an attitude is familiar to
every student of the eighteenth century, that age when
the similarities between Horace and Mr. Pope seemed
so much more striking than the differences, and when
etymologies told us not the distance a word had come
but the kinship it could assert with other tongues not
yet regarded as dead. So in Trinity College Library the
busts of ancient and modern worthies look all of a
time; Demosthenes in particular has a strikingly Irish
look: you will see that face in the street outside. And to
live in a Dublin that maintained, in 1900, communica-
tions however attentuated with the Dublin of Swift
was to be exempt from any proto-Structuralist obliga-
tion to correct the excesses of the historical sense, because if you lived there you likely had no more historical sense than Swift had.

Hence the baffling ease with which Joycean destinies
can be deflected: as easily as an actor changes costume.
Bob Doran was doomed by checking into the wrong
boarding-house; Eveline must look toward a bitter life
because she met a man in a sailor-cap, playing a part.
This feel for the way things are is something Joyce
shares with Shakespeare, the only thing he really has in

The "Irish" Demosthenes

common with the poet who fascinated him above all
others: a sense that things are done in the world as they
are done in the theater, by changing garb and diction:
that different persons merely play different parts: that
young people try out parts, the parts available to them,
and get trapped in the last part they try out (the generic
Dubliners plot).

Accordingly no other novelist is so preoccupied
with clothes. The second sentence of *Ulysses* tells us
what Buck Mulligan is wearing, and lets us know that
in his yellow dressinggown he is playing at the morning rite of a priest in his chasuble. On the third page
Buck is calling Stephen "the loveliest mummer of
them all" [5/11]; on the fourth we learn that Stephen
wears Mulligan's boots and trousers (later Stephen
will imagine a Shakespearean actor dressed in "the
cast-off mail of a court buck" [188/188]). As Mulligan
rummages for the day's costume he mutters, "God,
we'll simply have to dress the character. I want puce
gloves and green boots" [17/23]. (Later we hear of
his "primrose elegance" [417/414].) Stephen wears a
"Hamlet hat." Bloom in nighttown passes through
innumerable changes of costume and idiom: idiom *is*
costume, for Joyce.

And as the elements of a costume cohere with one
another, so the coherence of adjacent words is with one
another. If we ask whether costume is appropriate to
wearer, we shall be reminded that the wearer's soul-
stuff may be a void to which the costume lends a look
of coherence, and if we ask whether the decorum of
words comports with that of their subject, level Irish
eyes will challenge us to produce a subject that exists
apart from the words. Bloom, was there a Bloom?
He is a shout in the street; a misprint makes him "L.

Boom" [647/568]. Joyce contrived that misprint. All is appearance, all. Joyce is never more thoroughly consistent than in his rejection of any Platonic truth we can imagine as real though disembodied. Your identity as you know it, that seems real: "But I, entelechy, form of forms, am I by memory because under everchanging forms" [189/190]. Who else, though, can know that?

This is something more than an eighteenth–century distrust in all but the evidential. During the 150 years that the rest of Europe, undergoing the prolonged experience we call Romanticism, was pursuing metaphors of growth and organic cohesion, we are not to imagine the Augustan certainties preserved in Ireland inviolate. No, certainty was leaking out of them; cynical acids were filling up the void from which certainty had been emptied; and in the Dublin James Joyce knew the aristocratic assurances which Yeatsian Platonism was trying to recreate with the aid of a mythical eighteenth century had in fact been transmuted into a nearly perfect Pyrrhonism: a whole community agreed upon this one thing, that no one at bottom knows what he is talking about because there is nothing to know except the talk.

The Irish as Joyce presents them (and who shall differ?) are such Pyrrhonists they are apt to be set snickering by the mere suspicion that an idea has entered the room. Pyrrhonisms's tactics have not varied since Sextus Empiricus exemplified them 1700 years before Bloomsday. They consist in pushing the dogmatizer into an infinite regress.

—But do you know what a nation means? says John Wyse.
—Yes, says Bloom.

—What is it? says John Wyse.

—A nation? says Bloom. A nation is the same people living in the same place.

—By God, then, says Ned, laughing, if that's so I'm a nation for I'm living in the same place for the past five years.

So of course everybody had a laugh at Bloom, and says he, trying to muck out of it:

—Or also living in different places.

—That covers my case, says Joe. [331/329–30]

"So of course everybody had a laugh at Bloom": nothing is more ridiculous than the man who thinks he knows what he is talking about.

—And the tragedy of it is, says the citizen, they believe it. The unfortunate yahoos believe it. [329/327]

"They" at this point are the English, and what they believe has something to do with the glorious British navy and civilization. The Citizen vents his passion on that idea:

—Their syphilisation, you mean, says the citizen. To hell with them! The curse of a goodfornothing God light sideways on the bloody thicklugged sons of whores' gets! No music and no art and no literature worthy of the name. Any civilisation they have they stole from us. Tonguetied sons of bastards' ghosts.

—The European family, says J.J. . . .

—They're not European, says the citizen. I was in Europe with Kevin Egan of Paris. You wouldn't see a trace of them or their language except in a *cabinet d'aisance*.

And says John Wyse:

—Full many a flower is born to blush unseen.

And says Lenehan that knows a bit of the lingo:

—*Conspuez les Anglais! Perfide Albion!* [325/323]

These passions, like hornets, select their victims with perfect impartiality. A few minutes later it is the turn of the French.

—The French! says the citizen. Set of dancing masters! Do you know what it is? They were never worth a roasted fart to Ireland. Aren't they trying to make a *entente cordiale* now at Tay Pay's dinnerparty with perfidious Albion? Firebrands of Europe and they always were.

—*Conspuez les Français,* says Lenehan, nobbling his beer.

—And as for the Prooshians and the Hanoverians, says Joe, haven't we had enough of those sausageeating bastards on the throne from George the Elector down to the German lad and the flatulent old bitch that's dead? [330/328–29]

And so on, to a discreditable anecdote about Queen Victoria being rolled into bed drunk; and so on, and on. All the political discourse in Barney Kiernan's pub comes down to name-calling, and we shall be mistaken if we brush it aside with remarks about ignorance and bigotry, which is but to parry name-calling by calling it more genteel names. It proceeds, this habit of Barney Kiernan's customers, from a coherent philosophical position, nowhere articulated because skepticism cannot acknowledge its dogmas: that *when statements can have no substance they can only have style*. The style, moreover, is the man. To destroy the one is the way to destroy the other. So you do not argue with people, as though there were any meaning to proving them "wrong." (Bloom never seems more ridiculous than when he argues.) You may hold a rhetorical contest, but that is Indian Wrestling and not the same thing as an argument. To make a really effective political point you blow something up, it scarcely matters what so long as it exists in some symbolic association with the object of your critique. It will have been an appearance, but nothing else is real. When the temperature of discourse is too low for shattered glass and toppling masonry, you confine yourself to savage stylistic dissection. Hence a civilization of remarks and personal appraisals, where time and again we are shown men bent over a piece of writing—a paean to Our Lovely Land, a hangman's letter of application—to test its resonances, or men listening to a piece of formal discourse the better to savor its figuration. "Belief" is a state in which unfortunate yahoos are caught. The superior man, the Houyhnhnm one is tempted to say, does not incline toward belief but practices assessment. What he assesses is surface and style.

As does Joyce's reader, who is apt to be finding Mr. Bloom deficient in style. Catching sight of birds, Bloom is visited by a poetical moment:

> *The hungry famished gull*
> *Flaps o'er the waters dull.*

That is how poets write, the similar sounds. But then Shakespeare has no rhymes: blank verse. The flow of the language it is. The thoughts. Solemn.

> *Hamlet, I am thy father's spirit*
> *Doomed for a certain time to walk the earth.*[152/152]

We are quick (aren't we?) to recognize the device: Flaubertian Received Ideas, concatenated. Our cue is to smile. And yet it is not really at the substance of Mr. Bloom's ideas that we smile; rhyme has an honorable history as a finding device for meanings. We may remember that we are to compare the earlier meditations of Stephen Dedalus on the same topic, and though Stephen is hyper-literary, flypapered in literature, it is not evident that he carries the analysis any deeper:

Mouth, south. Is the mouth south someway? Or the south a mouth? Must be some. South, pout, out, shout, drouth. Rhymes: two men dressed the same, looking the same, two by two.

. . . . *la tua pace*
. . . . *che parlar ti piace*
. . . . *mentrechè il vento, come fa, si tace*

He saw them, three by three, approaching girls, in green, in rose, in russet, entwining *per l'aere perso* in mauve, in purple, *quella pacifica oriafiamma*, in gold or oriflame, *di rimirar fé piú ardenti*. But I old men, penitent, leadenfooted, underdarkneath the night: mouth, south: tomb, womb. [138/139]

Stephen quotes Dante, not Shakespeare, and (aided by Dante) he rhymes rhymes with girls and girls with colors. It is a more consummate performance altogether, cadenced and framed. But "Is the mouth south someway?" seems worthy of Bloom—if Bloomish questions are ridiculous all questions are†—and as for couplets as pairs of men dressed alike, if this points up a Bloomsday eyerhyme between himself and Bloom, two men in mourning, the credit for this is not Stephen's but the author's, just as it is the author, not Bloom, who has lent point to Bloom's claim to be Hamlet's father.

No, the mouth is not south some way, but there is a phenomenal plane on which *mouth* consorts with *south*. That *is* how poets write, the similar sounds: locating

---

†Thus Bloom's "Do fish ever get seasick?" [379/376] now has a scientific answer:

> *SEASICK FISH*
> Fish can get seasick if
> caught in heavy waves for an
> extended period of time.
> —Santa Barbara (Calif.) *News-Press*, July 6, 1975

and pinning down those hollow but indisputable re-
semblances, beneath which it does us no good whatever to enquire. A Pyrrhonist description of *The Divine Comedy* would note its vast inventory of interlocking similarities, most evidently its interlocking
sounds, and observe that whatever else Dante's poem
may be it is certainly a vast adduction of words that
come in threes: the Italian dictionary, so to speak,
reorganized to display resources of triple rhyme.

This parody of a Structuralist description unhitches
what is discoverable in the poem from all history
that came before the poem, including the history of
Trinitarian theology that conferred such virtue upon
threes. It is by removing history, confining yourself to
the present instant—as to 16 June 1904—that you produce odd effects of that order. When Gulliver describes
English lawcourts to the Houyhnhnms, and the
Houyhnhnms decide on the evidence he has presented
that the courts exist to persecute the unfortunate, there
is no way to answer them without evoking history:
explaining what the law was intended for and asserting
that its intention does persist though things go wrong
in practice. But Swift is already playing the Pyrrhonist
game; he contrives that there is no way history can be
evoked, principally because Gulliver knows none. So
the Houyhnhnms cannot be answered. Similarly there
is no way to confer meaning on Dante's threes except
by invoking an intellectual history which you must
produce from your sleeve because the poem (here,
now) cannot contain it. And *Ulysses* teems with
analogies of theme and contour on which likewise
there is no way to confer meaning except by adducing
what *Ulysses* cannot contain: the intellectual past
which is not in the mind of anyone in the book.

We can see Joyce acknowledging the troublesome logic of his book in what seems to have been virtually the last act he performed on it, the deletion of the Homeric chapter headings which are plainly written on the Rosenbach manuscript: Telemachus, Nestor, Proteus . . . . We are so used to these headings we easily forget that the book nowhere contains them. They had to be supplied from outside, and Joyce was put to considerable trouble to manipulate an *ad hoc* critical tradition which should supply them and lend them currency. He needed to confer a look of meaning on his vast structure of analogies and coincidences; and meaning, however much its evidence inheres, on Pyrrhonist principles cannot itself inhere. He permitted himself one extraneous element only, attached to the book itself: one word of seven letters: the title: *Ulysses.* That title we may describe as an auctorial comment, the sole *remark* the author (otherwise invisible, paring his fingernails) permits himself amid a quarter-million words. It is as though he had decided to retitle the last story in *Dubliners,* not "The Dead" but "Orpheus."

For between the Christmastime story and the Bloomsday novel there is this fascinating analogy, that within each work people give partial and misleading explanations, while the reader, stationed outside the work, can give another of which the fictive personnel have no inkling. Gabriel Conroy adduces the Three Graces, and the Judgment of Paris. The "correct" myth is that of Orpheus. Stephen Dedalus adduces Hamlet, Leopold Bloom adduces Don Giovanni. The "correct" myth is that of Ulysses.

Correct?

A criterion of correctness: whoever agrees that "The

Dead" reenacts the story of Orpheus and Eurydice is
assenting to a satisfactory neatness of fit, moreover an
economy, an elegance, which aligns a redundancy of
particulars, much as two redundant rows of columns
in Bernini's elliptical colonnade in Rome align themselves and magically disappear behind the members of
the front row the moment we are standing on the right
spot. The effect is instantaneous, absolute as Euclid;
we should have no doubt that the spot had been desig-
nated by Bernini even if a metal plate in the pavement
did not mark it. And the title "Orpheus," affixed to
"The Dead," would resemble that metal plate.

Unlike "The Dead," *Ulysses* does come equipped
with a metal plate, the title, to tell us where to stand if
we desire certain simplifications. We may guess that
there were many reasons for Joyce to have let the title
stand even though he deleted the chapter headings.
One reason is the enormous complexity of the book,
permitting as it does so many trial alignments we
might never be sure we had the right one. Another is
the imperfection of the Homeric parallel: one episode,
The Wandering Rocks, is not in Homer at all, and
many are taken out of sequence, and the whole second
half of the *Odyssey*, Odysseus' dealings with the
suitors, has no counterpart in *Ulysses* because Joyce has
in effect folded it over the first half—Bloom dealing
with Boylan all day by simply getting used to the idea
of him. Had the title been suppressed like the headings,
and had some ingenious scholar many years later ar-
gued in *PMLA* that Homeric structures seemed recoverable from *Ulysses*, it is easy to imagine how over-
whelming the counter-arguments would seem.

We find Ulysses in *Ulysses* because the author told us
to. The Author of the Bible, correspondingly, told

men what to find in the history He had arranged. God, we may posit, worked freely. Joyce was trapped in a consequence of the principle he presents as pervading Dublin, the principle that all cohesion is of the surface, all reality stylistic, all decorum cosmetic. In supplying us with a title and then with some authorized exegesis, he was compelled to assert an arbitrary proposition, that the hidden cohering principle of the book was simply what the author said it was: the author who, be it remembered, must be supposed not to exist. Like fatherhood in Stephen's exposition, authorship must be presumed to be a mystical estate, from only begetter to only begotten; and on that mystery, like the Church Stephen expounds, the book "is founded and founded irremoveably because founded like the world, macro- and microcosm, upon the void. Upon incertitude, upon unlikelihood" [207/207].

One last step. Joyce was the great master of anti-climax, the Michelangelo of the grotesque, the artist whose possessing theme is men's inability to sustain heroic conceptions. His countryman W. B. Yeats willed himself to sustain them: Yeats whose interest in reincarnation enabled him to see Maud Gonne on a Dublin soapbox as wilful Helen, Helen returned but deprived of a Troy to burn. Occasionally Joyce moved in Yeatsian circles: *Ulysses* records a visit of Stephen's to A. E., seeking light and borrowing a pound. Joyce later played down his interest in mystics' light to the point of invisibility. Yet it was surely at the behest of talk in Dawson Chambers about metempsychosis (Molly Bloom's "met him pikehoses" [154/153]) and by analogy with Maud Gonne as Helen returned that he conceived Bloom as unwitting Ulysses.

But Helen enhances Maud; Ulysses does not enhance Bloom. How Bloom is enhanced is another topic, pertaining to the sheer energy of presentation, energy which renders Bloom's unflagging alertness and animates the detailed tug of his plight on our human sympathies. But to guess, or to learn from the title, or from Joyce's letters, that Bloom is Ulysses unawares does not raise him to heroic stature. Inspected (and we are dissuaded from inspecting it) this knowledge either turns Bloom into a caricature or turns Homer into a romantic. Either Bloom cannot bend that bow (and he does not bend it) or Homer overrated its strength.

One thing Joyce was up to, we may entertain ourselves by guessing, was a practical joke on the Yeatsians, the most elaborate practical joke in the history of letters. Midway through the text we even hear Yeats burbling, "The most beautiful book that has come out of our country in my time. One thinks of Homer" [216/216]. It is as though Yeats had been trapped into writing a blurb for a book Joyce knew he would detest (and in fact Yeats never finished reading it).

And yet one *does* think of Homer; one must, if the book is to work: if, even taking the book on its least noble level, the joke on Yeats is to work. There is no way out of that logic. Our final image may well be of Dedalus, who built a labyrinth to prevent the Minotaur from escaping and then himself could not escape, because so long as he alone knew the secret the island had itself become a labyrinth, confining him.

So he was spurred to new invention, and disappeared straight up, into the sky.

The trouble Joyce took to get *Ulysses* explicated while making the explications seem to come from other men resembles Dedalus' trouble over his wings:

a contrivance to negate the side-effects of an over-successful contrivance. It is behind Valery Larbaud and Stuart Gilbert and Frank Budgen that the artist disappears, nail-file in hand. It was they, at his behest, who equipped the great affirmation of meaninglessness with meaning. We have been carrying on their work ever since, coupling Pyrrho with Plato as though it were the most natural coupling in the world. And Joyce, despite the most diligent biographical effort, has meanwhile ascended on unexpected wings into the air and out of sight.

4. Beyond Objectivity

—Out of sight, but not out of earshot: his voices people the novel's space. Voices? "The narrative voice" is a convention of commonsense criticism; need there be more? Apparently; for Homer, who knew more than common sense knows about storytelling, found that he could not get a story told without at a minimum two voices, his own and the Muse's (one reason *Ulysses* ends with a woman speaking).

Joyce was Homer's scrupulous apprentice. It was Homer, we've seen, who held his wild book together, to an extent he acknowledged in dropping his pretense of nonexistence long enough to affix the enigmatic title. Year after year, explaining what he was up to, he commenced his explanation to this or that newcomer not with Bloom nor with Dublin but with the *Odyssey*. His chisel was set, that meant, to the hardest stone: his way was Homer's way, confronting a subject like Homer's.

This needs stressing. The handy word "myth," as in Eliot's "*Ulysses*, Order and Myth," is simply wrong, an uninspected legacy from the age of Matthew Arnold and Max Müller.★ True, readers of Homer were agreed in the 1860's that the story he told had no basis in fact worth pursuing, had even perhaps condensed out of a solar myth, and when Schliemann set out to find Troy he looked wondrous naive, like a seeker after planks of the Ark atop Ararat. But twelve years before

Joyce was born he did find Troy, and he did excavate golden masks from Homer's "golden Mycenae," and soon other spades were busy turning over dust indistinguishable from Odysseus's and Helen's. If there was one thing of which James Joyce was thoroughly convinced when he took up the story, with on his bookshelf a long work by a French scholar retracing Odysseus's voyages through the Mediterranean, it was that whatever the *Odyssey* may have been it was certainly not a "myth." It told of a man who lived and fought and voyaged, a man not imagined by Homer but appropriated and recreated by the imagination of Homer, much as Joyce himself proposed to recreate a Dublin odd-jobs entrepreneur, reputedly of Jewish ancestry, who went under the name of Mr. Hunter. Whatever we do not know about Mr. Hunter we can be sure he was real. Joyce mentions his name in a letter to his brother Stanislaus in a casual way that leaves no doubt he thought Stannie would know who was meant. The mention occurs in the course of a proposal to write a story called "Ulysses." Ulysses was real too.

So what had Homer done with the story? He had begun by asking the Muse to help him, and not help him make the story up but help him tell it. For his access to Homer, Joyce, with no classical Greek, is said to have relied on fairly business-like translations, Cowper's and Butler's,* but at least the first line of the Greek he carried in his memory: on one convivial occasion he wrote it out to caption a sketch of Bloom. Its first four words are Ἄνδρα μοι ἔννεπε Μοῦσα, naming in sequence three persons: *andra,* the man, Odysseus; *moi,* the singer, Homer; *Mousa,* the Muse, the authority. Homer's is the voice we first hear, but what he tells us about that man the Muse must tell him. It is she who knows, and he who words her knowledge; or does he simply voice her words? A scholiast would be bold indeed who would venture to mark the moment in the text at which Homer's narration is taken up by hers. He knows something of the story, but not enough to tell it unaided; is it the information he lacks, or the afflatus? Anyhow he knows the circumstances of the hero at the point where he directs the Muse to begin. Robert Fitzgerald catches the uncatchability of the transition:

> Begin when all the rest who left behind them
> headlong death in battle or at sea
> had long ago returned, while he alone still hungered
> for home and wife. Her ladyship Kalypso
> clung to him in her sea-hollowed caves—
> who craved him for her own. . . .

Where does Homer's prompting cease and the flow of the divine narrative commence? And does he ever wholly retire?

A more practical question is why the Muse is needed, and what her presence has to teach a modern writer. It depends which Homer we ask. Our most up-to-date Homer, Parry and Lord's "oral-formulaic" improvisor, may be disregarded since he was invented too late for Joyce to have heard of him (his answer would doubtless be that the Muse is the power who enables you to improvise several thousand hexameters on your feet at a go without getting stuck). The stained-glass Homer of Butcher and Lang commences "Tell me, Muse, of that man, so ready at need," because gentlemen inaugurate momentous things with prayer; but while Joyce sometimes felt like a Victorian engineer and compared work on *Finnegans Wake* to tunnelling through a mountain, he was unattracted by the role of Victorian gentleman. His Homer was such a workmanlike realist as Samuel Butler intuited (unencumbered, though, by Butler's coat-trailing about a Sicilian princess), and for such a Homer the use of a Muse is twofold. She can preside over elevations of style as they are needed; and she can share thematic knowledge with the author, who need no longer occupy that monocular "point of view" where Henry James was often so cramped.

For the occupant of a "point of view" is like a *voyeur* (how can he possibly have known?) while the events of the *Odyssey* are public property, in their main outlines known to everyone (like anything at all in Dublin). As Homer and the Muse and, yes, the audience all know the story of Odysseus, and the thing to be concentrated on is the texture of today's retelling, so all Dublin invariably knows who was just drinking with whom and what they quarrelled about, and many voices are free to address themselves to the work of elaboration, the most talented bearing the more intricate rhetorical burdens. Perhaps Joyce's sense of things was not as far from the oral–formulaic as chronology might have led us to suppose.

He commences *Ulysses*, anyhow, as a sort of duet for two narrators, or perhaps a conspiracy between them. The doubleness he owes to Homer, and later his mischievous logical mind will have improvements to offer on what Homer suggests. At present, though, atop the Martello Tower, an ambiguously double narrator suffices: one voice perhaps better informed about stage-management, the other a more accomplished lyrical technician.

In the first episode, accordingly—wait, things are

more complicated still. There is yet one more person present: a twentieth-century presence, the novel-reading reader, the creation of the books he has read already and now confronting one more new book. What the reader expects, in this first episode, controls much of what the first narrator can do. For the arts create their audiences who then control them, and as the Noh-goer was shaped by one kind of theater and Shakespeare's groundling by another kind, so the early twentieth-century novel-reader (by no means extinct today but greatly mutated) may be described as a complex of expectations and agreements-to-respond that has been shaped by Edwardian fiction, its contrivances, climaxes, "rattling good stories," above all by its unobtrusive novelese, the language Joseph Conrad and Ford Madox Hueffer steeled themselves daily not to write.

This language, not some unthinkable "objective" metalanguage, is what the first narrator of "Telemachus" employs as he moves characters about and reports their gestures. If we have difficulty noticing it, that is because certain narrative assumptions have changed little since 1904. To the inhabitant of a period the characterizing idiom of that period, whether in painting, in sculpture or in literature, is absolutely invisible.* It took Conrad—a Pole, Joyce—a Dubliner, and Hueffer—who would rather have been writing in French—to detect Edwardian novelese accurately enough to avoid it, or (in Joyce's case) to use it deliberately before avoiding it deliberately.

It is by no means a contemptible idiom. It does not like "Nausicaa" novelese, strain after portentousness ("But who was Gerty?" [348/346]). Its mannerisms, not easy to catalogue, include a certain fussiness about setting and decor (much "up" and "down" and "across" [5/11]; much particularity of "jagged granite" and shafts of light meeting amid turning coalsmoke); a tendency toward longer speeches than later conventions would think plausible in casual dialogue; a predilection for eloquent dumbshow ("Stephen suffered him to pull out and hold up on show by its corner a dirty crumpled handkerchief" [4/11]); and certain epithetic opulences we'll look at presently. The English novel's heritage from the English stage is appreciable here, though attenuated to a set of economical flourishes. It all suits "Telemachus," where everyone is acting: stage-Irishman, stage-Englishman, stage-poet.

So the style of "Telemachus," called in the famous schema "Narrative (young)," today gives off here and there an unmistakeable ring of Edwardian novelese.

At the time only Wyndham Lewis noticed this ring, enabled by the fact that having written *The Enemy of the Stars* in 1914 he was already living in an idiom of the future; and Lewis as so often drew the wrong conclusion, that there was, despite all the huff and puff of modernity, something *old-fashioned* about Mr. Joyce's methods. We have seen Lewis fail to define the Uncle Charles Principle even in identifying traces of its working; he scored another near-miss in spotting traces of the kind of novel in which Dedalus and Mulligan imagine they are characters, while not noticing that such traces do not extend beyond the first episode. See him respond to the traces of theater:

Mulligan asks the hero for his handkerchief. 'Stephen *suffered* him to pull out' the handkerchief, etc. The word 'suffered' and the bathos of the gesture involved in the offering of the pocket, are characteristic.

Buck Mulligan 'turned abruptly *his great searching eyes*

from the sea,' etc. Great searching eyes! Oh, where were the
great searching eyes of the author, from whom no verbal
cliché may escape, when he wrote that? . . .

'"Then what is it?" Buck Mulligan asked impatiently.
"Cough it up." Stephen freed his arm quietly.' Stephen does
everything 'quietly,' whether he 'quietly' touches Mulligan
on the arm or 'quietly' frees his own. He is a very quiet man
indeed. . . .

"Great searching eyes" [5/11] is indeed a saliency;
we mentioned epithetic opulences, and this is one: an
Uncle Charles deformation of the language by the
proximity of Mulligan, as "quietly" [7/14] is a deformation effected by that of Stephen. Such words respond to the way the young men see themselves, in a
chapter where everything touches on roles and costumes, the very "gunrest" [3/9] a circular center-stage.
Mulligan-style and Stephen-style moreover blend
with a set of narrative mannerisms which constitute
novel-style and license such phrases as, in the very first
sentence, "bearing a bowl" [3/9]. (In novelese whatever could have been *carried* is apt to be *borne;* another
Joyce character just commencing to see himself as a fictive personage, the boy in "Araby," imagined "that I
bore my chalice safely through a throng of foes," and
Mulligan's verb like Mulligan's stance appears to recall this. But Mulligan if he is Oliver Gogarty's age is
perhaps sixteen years older than that boy was, and the
verb touches him the way he plays the part, cynically.)
One voice then in this episode is moving characters
about, and reporting their doings, in fluent unempha-
tic novelese, barely to be distinguished from a neutral
idiom save by occasional "great searching eyes," an
occasional "strong wellknit trunk" ("Laughter seized

all his strong wellknit trunk" [6/12]). Still it *is* an idiom however we characterize it: the voice of someone trying phrases to himself as he writes down a story. No "objective" style, Joyce is already hinting, can in truth be discovered to exist, no registration of so–many–things–almost–in–an–equal–number–of–words; an attempt to simulate one will itself be a style, a narrator's role.

And while the first voice attends to the chapter's housekeeping, a second narrative voice is uttering passages like the following:

Woodshadows floated silently by through the morning peace from the stairhead seaward where he gazed. Inshore and farther out the mirror of water whitened, spurned by lightshod hurrying feet. White breast of the dim sea. The twining stresses, two by two. A hand plucking the harpstrings merging their twining chords. Wavewhite wedded words shivering on the dim tide. [9/15]

Fulfilling one office of the Muse in periodically elevating the style, this second narrator has served an apprenticeship on *A Portrait of the Artist as a Young Man* and become a virtuoso of the Uncle Charles Principle: the narrative idiom bent by a person's proximity as a star defined by Einstein will bend passing light. The only person on the parapet now is Stephen. These thoughts of woodshadows floating are not Stephen's, not quite, but the sentences that brush them in absorb Stephenwords and Stephen–rhythms, moving us imperceptibly into Stephen's thoughts:

A cloud began to cover the sun slowly, shadowing the bay in deeper green. It lay behind him, a bowl of bitter waters.

Fergus' song: I sang it alone in the house, holding down the long dark chords. [9/15]

Only if we catch the shift from third person to first are we assured that we have left the outside for the inside: are now in Stephen's mind, where "holding down the long dark chords" has a self-approving expressiveness. Inside Stephen's mind, where self-appreciation reigns, is a less blithe zone than the penumbra commanded by the dextrous second narrator, whose facility is Protean, whose responsibility is to the sensation reported rather than to the locked and cherished phrase, and whose deftness is seemingly incomparable. He and Stephen, with practice, are readily differentiated. It is Stephen who hears the squeal of his ashplant's ferrule on the path as "My familiar, after me, calling Steeeeeeeeeeeephen" [20/26], and it was on finicky Stephen's behalf that Joyce instructed the printer to put in 12 e's (except for the printer of the Rosenbach facsimile, no printer until this moment has ever obliged). It is the second narrator who manages such passing triumphs of narrative economy as the emergence of the elderly swimmer:

An elderly man shot up near the spur of rock a blowing red face. He scrambled up by the stones, water glistening on his pate and on its garland of grey hair, water rilling over his chest and paunch and spilling jets out of his sagging black loincloth. [22/28]

—how exact that twinned *rilling* and *spilling*!

This second narrator, vivid narrator, Muse, flaunts skills such as Stephen covets, hence a somewhat misleading likeness to Stephen's idiom. To perceive him clearly we must wait till Stephen is offstage and the only person present is Leopold Bloom. Then we shall recognize the virtuoso whose miracles of one-word *naming* we've already discussed, sharing narrative control with a less flamboyant craftsman whose Uncle Charles sensibilities respond to the pressure of Bloom's presence, and who takes us deftly in and out of Bloom's mind.

Kidneys were on his mind as he moved about the kitchen softly, righting her breakfast things on the humpy tray. Gelid light and air were in the kitchen but out of doors gentle summer morning everywhere. Made him feel a bit peckish. [55/57]

Here the two voices are just distinguishable. "Peckish," from the notation of Bloom's feelings, is a Bloom-word, but "gelid," responsive to the ambient light, is not. It is not even a word we should expect Bloom to know, any more than he would know words like *rhododaktylos*, which pertain to Homeric evocations of light. Joyce here offers the first signallings of what we've described as a technique for *separating* Bloom's thoughts from the narrative gestures.

These two narrators command different vocabularies and proceed according to different canons. At the outset their command is evenly matched, and the first three Bloom episodes, culminating in "Hades," exhibit an economical weaving of inner and outer, the brisk notations of Bloom's thought and the wonderfully compact narration glinting against one another. Thus when Bloom is in search of a secluded place to read his clandestine letter, we are told:

With careful tread he passed over a hopscotch court with its forgotten pickeystone. Not a sinner. Near the timberyard a squatted child at marbles, alone, shooting the taw with a cunnythumb. A wise tabby, a blinking sphinx, watched

from her warm sill. Pity to disturb them. Mohammed cut a
piece out of his mantle not to wake her. Open it. And once I
played marbles when I went to that old dame's school. [77/
78–79]

Here Bloom and narration receive equal time, equal
emphasis. As we have come to expect, the textures are
kept distinct: *pickeystone, squatted, taw, cunnythumb*—
four unique words in two lines—and the elegantly
enjambed construction "a wise tabby, a blinking
sphinx," these are narrator's mannerisms; "Pity to disturb them" is unmistakeably Bloom's (and the uncertain referent of "them"—child or cat?—is James
Joyce's). So it is in "Calypso," "Lotus Eaters,"
"Hades."

But a little past the hundredth page we have our first
intimation that one of the two narrators, the one responsible for the external world, is getting impatient.
This narrator, all vividness in his purview, has had a
few fine moments just previously, achieving for instance a concise impression of Bloom's stroll alone
through the cemetery:

Mr Bloom walked unheeded along the grove by saddened
angels, crosses, broken pillars, family vaults, stone hopes
praying with upcast eyes, old Ireland's hearts and hands.
[113/114]

Now, clamping his teeth on the bit, he offers the following on the first page of "Aeolus":

Grossbooted draymen rolled barrels dullthudding out of
Prince's stores and bumped them up on the brewery float.
On the brewery float bumped dullthudding barrels rolled
by grossbooted draymen out of Prince's stores. [116/118]

He also, with a certain malicious eye for the malap-ropos, pastes captions across the page throughout the text of this episode. This narrator is letting us know that he is there, and that he will not necessarily remain content to serve the needs of the narrative, even sup-posing the improbable, that its needs can be simply defined. No, he is *reading* the narrative, and reserves the privilege of letting us know what he thinks of it. There is nothing about which he can be more "objective" than about his own performance, and whenever the performance undertakes self-scrutiny the effect is far-cical. ("Grossbooted draymen rolled barrels dullthud-ding . . . :" hark to the dullthudding onamatopoeia! Then run it backwards.) He is taking his cue from editor and chums in the *Evening Telegraph* office, who are paying no heed at all to putting out a newspaper, though it is somehow getting put out. What they are doing is subjecting bits of oratory to stylistic com-ment, Pyrrhonism's dearest ritual. So the second nar-rator, an invisible presence, notes Professor McHugh twanging a bit of dental floss and deftly accords this event a caption: "O, HARP EOLIAN" [127/129].

He is an ironic, malicious figure, this second nar-rator: a counterpart of the fate that presides over the universe of farce, arranging the strategic presence of banana peels or helping weave the network of coinci-dence that enmeshes impartially the victims of Thomas Hardy's President of the Immortals and the frantic stage couples in three adjacent French bed-rooms. He has written a great many books before this one, he will have us know, and arranged a great many pantomimes. *The Comedy of Errors* is a mobile of his contrivance. Objectivity, so naively taken for ultimate truth, was a game he invented, and he prompted the

malicious Swift to elaborate its rules to the end that
the ironic Flaubert, undreamed-of by Swift, might
employ them to entrap on paper the soul of Charles
Bovary, of whom it is recorded that after his death the
doctors opened him up and found nothing.

He is the spirit who nudged Stephen Dedalus, in
another book, to fling his hand high in declamation
and then later reflect that he must have looked like a
fellow flinging a handful of peas into the air (*that*, if you
like, is an objective look). And with whatever precaution the rules of probability and causality may be
framed in this new book *Ulysses*, he will have us know
that he does not propose to be bound by them. He
makes fun of the interlocking of motifs, setting down
in the midst of Bloom's meditations in "Sirens" a sentence from Stephen's discourse on Shakespeare which
(commentators keep noting with some perplexity)
Bloom was not present to hear. We deduce, for what
good it may do us, that such a manoeuver is permitted
in this chapter; in the previous chapter, "Wandering
Rocks," extraneous material could be introduced only
into a vignette to which it was bound by synchronic-
ity. He also makes fun of the coolly "objective" opening of the book's second part, "Mr Leopold Bloom ate
with relish the inner organs of beasts and fowls" [55–
56/57], and when Bloom many hours later sits down to
a dish of inner organs with Richie Goulding (of Collis
& Ward, solicitors), he enjoys reminding us that back
in its seemingly more responsible phase the narrative
had uttered a statement that seemed pointless at the
time:*

Pat served uncovered dishes. Leopold cut liverslices. As said
before he ate with relish the inner organs, nutty gizzards,
fried cod's roes while Richie Goulding, Collis, Ward ate

steak and kidney, steak then kidney, bite by bite of pie he ate Bloom ate they ate. [269/268]

And again, a page later, "Bloom ate liv as said before" [271/270]. (And what does "with relish" mean? With enjoyment, or with condiments? The most specifying language proves porous.)

Meanwhile the other narrator tries to get on with the business of the book, arranging for instance Bloom's thoughts into patterns we are familiar with. The integrity of Bloom's inner monologue, that alone seems immune to monkey-business.

But not immune to suppression. After "Sirens" comes "Cyclops," and throughout "Cyclops" we hear nothing of Bloom's thoughts at all, only a few of his spoken words. Does this mean he is at last presented "objectively"? Not at all; for the second narrator has taken over completely, which is as though the Royal Mint had been commandeered by the Artful Dodger. Thoroughly bored with his assigned role as miniaturist of vivid descriptive bits, the second narrator is giving an expansive impersonation of a Dublin barfly, anonymous (like any narrator) and adrip with garrulous malice. "Old sheepsface" [345/343], he calls Bloom, and "old lardyface" [333/331], and other things more intricate and less complimentary. This barfly is the only *personified* narrator in the entire book, which is a way of saying that this episode alone is imparted through the cadence of speech, except when the impersonator, surpassing himself and perhaps remembering his caper with the headlines in "Aeolus," interrupts his own logorrhea with parodies, chiefly of newspaper clippings.

Having gotten this out of his system, our unbridled virtuoso next tries what he can do with a written idiom. Taking a quick glance at his assigned subject, three girls on the beach, he plunges in with the practiced fluency that guided a thousand Victorian pens:

> The summer evening had begun to fold the world in its mysterious embrace. Far away in the west the sun was setting and the last glow of all too fleeting day lingered lovingly on sea and strand, on the proud promontory of dear old Howth guarding as ever the waters of the bay, . . . [346/344]

—everything, in short, going on as usual: Howth has not moved, nor the sun stayed in its course. He keeps this up for twenty pages, subjecting events as well as sensibilities to the coercions of this new style of his; so Bloom's watch proves to have stopped at the moment of Molly's adultery, just as it would have done were he a character in the kind of novel this style presupposes.★

Suddenly the prime narrator—absent now for so long, perhaps at supper—snatches the pen and transcribes fifteen nearly unbroken pages of Bloom's interior monologue, the last long stretch of it we shall ever encounter. We are almost exactly at the midpoint of the book.

But the second narrator has by now grown in power like the Sorcerer's Apprentice. He retrieves the pen, and proceeds to demonstrate the interesting proposition that it was he who shaped the whole of English literature from earliest times until now. During his recapitulation of this chore ("The Oxen of the Sun") Bloom and Stephen are barely visible and wholly inaudible. Much as in the crucial chapter of Bloom's cuckolding we were almost continually distracted by tricksy imitations of musical effects, so now in the crucial chapter when after two near misses—at the newspaper office, in the library—he and Stephen meet at last, we are debarred from scrutiny of either man's thoughts and prevented from hearing one word that is spoken by anybody, so enamored is the narrator of his system of stylistic impersonations. When late in the episode voices finally do break through, the first word is the name of a pub, spoken by Stephen; thereafter, assailed for five pages by nothing but voices, we can hardly make out whose they are or what they are saying. What is born in this birth-chapter, after forty paragraphs *in utero*, seems to be disembodied Speech, which promptly fills the universe with its yells.

And when, in the episode that follows, the longest by far in the book, typography assures us that we may expect ordered speeches at last—surely this is a play?—we find we are again being hoaxed, for we cannot be sure, reading speech after speech, what if anything was really said, what was only thought but not said, and what has been supplied by the second narrator as expressive substitute for words no one was obliging enough to speak or think.

So one way to describe the curious course of *Ulysses* from "Aeolus" to "Circe" is to plot the insolences of the second narrator, and it is easy to wish he would simply tell us what happened, like Gulliver telling of that famous morning in Lilliput.

We have seen, though, that Gulliver's empirical objectivity is a discipline for confining what is narrated within the experience of a single narrator. Since by strict construction this would permit only first-person narrative, it was eventually reinterpreted to yield the famous convention of the Point of View, employing a foreground character over whose shoulder auctorial infallibility permits us to look. As novelists grew more interested in the logic of their craft, Point of View exercised an increasing tyranny over narrative freedom, until a major part of the calculation of a Henry James was devoted to arranging events so that his viewpoint-character could have known of them.

And there is an odd consequence. When a writer's style tells us, like James's, that he is going about his work deliberately, then if he does find a first-person narrator convenient we are apt to cry Aha!, suspecting that a tricky purpose has been signalled, infallibility suspended, that we are to doubt the narrator's understanding (for who trusts a mere *person*?). "The Turn of the Screw" has prompted reams of controversy about the deluded governess, and Ford Madox Ford's *The Good Soldier* gets skewered by analogous suppositions: what a fool is the preposterous Dowell! How gauche to accept a version that comes from him! It is rather a relief to find Joyce so frankly deceptive. We at least needn't probe the second narrator's psyche; except when he's being the malevolent "Cyclops" barfly, he is no more than an explicator's fiction, projected from the book of many devices.

We can say, though, that he is Irish if not "all too Irish": a fluent performer, a touch malicious, and something of an amateur epistemologist: not a countryman of Jonathan Swift's for nothing and participant moreover in the considerable expertise of James Joyce, who was writing accomplished narrative when he was barely out of college, for instance that tricky story "Eveline." Joyce saw no reason why first-person narration should be the sole code for signalling some limitation of awareness, and "Eveline" (1904), his second published story, is his first not altogether reluctant deception. He must have been both resignedly and cheerfully aware that numerous readers would share Eveline's fantasy, would suppose that a sailor who has "fallen on his feet in Buenos Ayres" is credible, one who has bought a house there and is spending a holiday in a rented room in Ireland; who proposes moreover to take her back as his bride to that South American house, though for some reason not gone into they can't get married till they've gotten there. Eveline believes all this because "Frank"—what a perfect name!—has skilfully shaped his yarn by the penny romances from which she derives her sense of the plausible. Penny romances are the liturgy of the innocent. The reader believes such stuff—most readers seem to—by accepting as fact what seems to be the narrative base of the story and is really no more than a careful statement of what naive Eveline has accepted.

Part of the narrative skill has gone into shaping the story's perceived world in such a way as to communicate Eveline's pathos. Another part is occupied in bestowing commas and minutiae of diction—"He had fallen on his feet in Buenos Ayres [comma] he said [comma]"—with a legalistic precision that shall cast slight but erosive doubt on certain aspects of Eveline's sense of the real. This has required the most steely control of style, one part of the writer's mind checking on the activities of the other, and exemplifies—so early!—something characteristic of Joyce, something he did in a variety of modes including the mode of pastiche. Pastiche and parody, these are modes which test the limits of someone else's system of perception. Any "style" is a system of limits; pastiche ascribes the system to another person, and invites us to attend to its recirculating habits and its exclusions. That is why Joyce, the student of Dublin limits, turned to stylistic imitation so frequently. There is nothing in his work more remarkable than the poem in memory of Charles Stewart Parnell the recitation of which climaxes "Ivy Day in the Committee Room": the pathos genuine, the rhetoric frigid and ludicrous, falsity exposed in the very grief it expresses.

> In palace, cabin or in cot
>   The Irish heart where'er it be
> Is bowed with woe—for he is gone
>   Who would have wrought her destiny.

And "Mr Crofton said that it was a very fine piece of writing." Joyce knew there would be readers who would believe that.

He does similar things, in the latter part of *A Portrait of the Artist as a Young Man*, with the aspirations of Stephen Dedalus, combining into single stylistic moments such a doubleness of vision as, in the earlier *Stephen Hero*, had required him alternately to cite glowing bits of Stephen's essay (meant to carry conviction) and then to mock him as "this heaven-ascending essayist." That we get so much theory from Stephen and such meager practice, that is one way of defining certain limits; another is a prose that draws attention, at climactic moments, to the seeming paucity of its own store of words, fingered and refingered as the halves of sentences run first forward, then backward:

Her bosom was as a bird's soft and slight, slight and soft as the breast of some darkplumaged dove. But her long fair hair was girlish: and girlish, and touched with the wonder of mortal beauty, her face.

The long paragraph—those are but the two closing sentences—carries enough marks of the rhetorical exercise (the sort of thing Stephen might write on getting home) to convey limitations that don't mock but define. A girl stood in the water, and Stephen's excited mind turned her into a bird, then "a wild angel . . . an envoy from the fair courts of life." What the girl presumably saw was a young man staring at her. In "Nausicaa" Joyce would later give us both sides of a similar encounter. In the *Portrait*, where we get only Stephen's version of everything, the careful limitations of style serve to remind us that there might be other versions. Reality, Joyce learned early, does not answer to the "point of view," the monocular vision, the single ascertainable tone. A tone, a voice, is somebody's, a person's, and people are confined to being themselves, are Evelines, are Croftons, are Stephens.

"Some of my methods," Joyce later said, "are trivial; and some are quadrivial." At the very least, on the model of two-eyed men, reality exacted a doubling: in the earlier fictions, a double attitude, which *Ulysses* divides into a double narrator of whom one member has a repertory of impersonations. It seems evident after the event that nothing on the scale of *Ulysses* could have been written in the manner of *Dubliners* or the *Portrait*. About 1919, some five years into the work, Joyce was quite clear that it couldn't even be written in the manner in which he had started it. (Early drafts of "Cyclops," even, contain Bloom's interior monologue, and suggest an episode in the manner of, say, "Hades": a good flexible manner.) From the start he knew this at least, that the long book needed extensive effects of immediacy, inner as well as outer, to install us at once and apparently without mediation in the psychosensual reality of Dublin city and the vivid play of experiencing minds. Characters must have voices, spoken and unspoken, but the office of distancing and differentiating had to be entrusted to an auxiliary narrative voice which could not be the voice of any character since no character beholds the book's entire action. For it is part of the book's theme that many unrelated actions are going on, linked by a grand design which can afford no comfort to any of the protagonists, conscious as they are of boredom and isolation.

So two schemes of narration were needed, an inner and an outer; we've seen how deliberately Joyce doubled the narrator's role in the very first episode, an episode he left pretty much alone when he went back and elaborated so many of the others. And the grand design needed to come together without some puppeteer-narrator seeming aware of it: some knowing Thackeray to repack the puppets into the box, some Hardy to explain that the President of the Immortals had been having some sport. The grand design is a design of multiple misunderstandings; Bloom thinks for instance that Stephen is a Poet and Philosopher whom it is his own finest destiny to have brought home; Molly thinks she can look forward to a young lover, and also thinks she heard Bloom ask for an egg in bed. What a future all this points to!— especially since Stephen, so far as we can tell, has disappeared out of the universe. The book's way, bringing such themes together, is not to assert the whimsical will of a President of the Immortals, but to clown through various systems of local presentation, all cohesive, hence Styles, and all wrong.

We should here reflect that wrongness and deception permeated the book back when its doings seemed
under the control of the characters, long before a
troublesome Stylist was usurping the foreground. The
first usurper (Stephen says) was Mulligan; there were
things he and Stephen weren't saying to each other; in
particular, Stephen wasn't saying that he didn't plan to
stay any longer, though "I will not sleep here tonight"
[23/29] was among his unvoiced thoughts. (Where will
he sleep? And who'll buy Mulligan's drinks?) As for
the Blooms, they evade each other like mad from the
first encounter we witness.

> —Who are the letters for?
> He looked at them. Mullingar. Milly.
> —A letter for me from Milly, he said carefully, and a card
> to you. And a letter for you.
> He laid her card and letter on the twill bedspread near the
> curve of her knees.
> —Do you want the blind up?
> Letting the blind up by gentle tugs halfway his backward
> eye saw her glance at the letter and tuck it under her pillow.
> [61–62/64]

"Carefully" is a word to note: Bloom's way of
negotiating minefields. So is "for": she asks "Who are
the letters for?" when she clearly means "from." And
the letter addressed "Mrs Marion" in a "bold hand"
[61/63] slides under the pillow. He knows this. She
knows he knows it. Later:

> A strip of torn envelope peeped from under the dimpled
> pillow. In the act of going he stayed to straighten the
> bedspread.
> —Who was the letter from? he asked.
> Bold hand. Marion.

—O, Boylan, she said. He's bringing the programme.

—What are you singing?

—*La ci darem* with J. C. Doyle, she said, and *Love's Old Sweet Song*. [63/65]

This states the convention, that when Boylan comes what goes on will be musical. They both know differently. When that hour arrives, a gratuitousness of music will bewilder both Bloom and the reader. And at just about that hour, when divers styles commence to screen what is happening, Bloom commences on a sequence of doings he's evasive about with himself and will be downright untruthful about when he gets home to Molly (who has meanwhile been being downright unfaithful to him).

"Sirens" to "Circe," these episodes span events he will never discuss with her and about which he is less than frank with himself. They include: her adultery, his letter to Martha, his ignominious flight from Kiernan's pub, his onanism on the beach, his trip to Nighttown. And though nothing discreditable happened at the lying-in hospital he suppresses it also, because his presence there conflicts with an alternative version of the hours in question according to which (as he later sleepily informs the sleepy but suspicious Molly) he went to see *Leah*, supped with Stephen at Wynn's, and brought home a Stephen injured not by a soldier's blow outside Bella Cohen's but by "a falsely calculated movement in the course of a postcenal gymnastic display" [735/656] (that's a part of his narrative one would wish to hear). And the episodes that prevarication screens from Molly are the same ones the second narrator's perversity imperfectly screens from us.

It is doubtful how far Molly is really deceived; for instance we are to learn that she has guessed about the correspondence with Martha, and also suspects that Poldy has been to Nighttown. But Homer's Ulysses was famous for lies, and communication between Joyce's Ulysses and his Penelope occurs chiefly around and under the words they speak. So one of the book's norms is the pack of lies by which husband and wife more or less keep in touch. The only words we can be sure have deceived Molly are ones Bloom will never remember speaking: "roc's auk's egg in the night of the bed . . ." [737/658], he muttered as he drifted down into sleep, and Molly misheard: "Yes because he never did a thing like that before as ask to get his breakfast in bed with a couple of eggs . . ." [738/659]. Later she makes plans for daybreak marketing; "then Ill throw him up his eggs and tea in the moustache-cup" [780/781]; and if she does Bloom will be mightily surprised. What brought *that* about? He will surely think she is penitent. Incipit, possibly, vita nuova, founded on a misheard mutter.

So deceiving Molly is part of the ritual for communicating with her, and deceiving Bloom a way of giving him messages ("I'm lonely, bored"). Deceiving the reader becomes, by a disconcerting extension, a way of establishing something about this book, about books, about life. For we are deceived, rather frequently, and there have even been canonical deceptions the righting of which constitutes much of the history of *Ulysses* criticism. Thus the first impression the book gave was that it was formless, which is what you'd think if you just turned through it with *Anna Karenina* in mind (or even *Tristram Shandy*, which is like itself wherever you sample it). The more interesting deceptions come from mistaking the import of unequivocal words, and are like supposing that Frank has a house for Eveline in Buenos Ayres because a

sentence seems to say he has. Thus reading the answer
to the famous question, "What preceding series?" we
easily imagine the improbable, that Molly has taken
twenty-five men at least into her bed, including "an
Italian organgrinder, an unknown gentleman in the
Gaiety Theatre," and "a bootblack at the General Post
Office" [731/652]. Critical consensus has been fifty
years deciding that this is nothing but a list of
Leopold's suspicions and that Boylan is probably her
first. A mere list doesn't tell us what it's a list of.

That's a major example, affecting our whole sense of
Poldy and Molly. More trivial examples abound. We
may think that we heard Molly say "met him pikehoses" (we did not), or that we were present when she
dealt out cards on bedclothes where the cat snuggled
(we were not). We are sure to think we have seen more
than we have, accompanied Bloom longer than we
have, for instance gone with him to the bath (we did
not; and unless we're very alert we're apt to suppose
the bath was Turkish); certainly that we've understood
more than we have. Evidence is deceptive, such mis-
adventures admonish; memory is tricky, notation can
be ambiguous, styles are provisional systems of consistency. (The style of "Ithaca," seemingly final in its
omniscience, that was what made us misread the list of
Molly's "lovers"; yet "Ithaca" is so responsive to
Bloom's wishes as to offer a budget he has evidently
falsified—where is the eleven shillings he left behind in
the whorehouse?—and its author had already rejected
a theology presented in an analogous style.)

The prototype of our difficulties with evidence is
"Wandering Rocks," where the second narrator is
explicitly in charge. Here "Mr Bloom's dental windows" [250/249] pertaining to a dentist Bloom unconnected with Leopold, have turned up in handbooks

ever since Stuart Gilbert's day as a specimen hazard to navigation, and they are but its publicized tip; as we tack amid the rocks we may at any moment grind keel on one of the "reader-traps" so numerous Mr. Clive Hart has arranged them in four types.★ That chapter, the tenth of eighteen, constitutes notice that deceit or attempted deceit are entailed in the ritual for communicating Bloomsday events to us.

For "outer" and "inner" are artifacts alike, artifacts of language; and this, it seems to have occurred to Joyce midway, was something the book had better acknowledge. He composed "Wandering Rocks," then backtracked and revised "Aeolus" to commence the acknowledgment there.

We are on ground contiguous to the ground people tread when they argue that "Lycidas" is insincere. For sincerity—Joyce is telling us—can damn. Not long before he blew his brains out Ernest Hemingway recalled how decades earlier in Paris he had used to overcome writer's block: "Do not worry," he would say to himself. "You have always written before and you will write now. All you have to do is write one true sentence. Write the truest sentence that you know." Remembering where this led can give one the shivers. By the time he'd used up the true sentences that he knew (how many does anyone know?) he was getting famous, and the enterprise of *being* Ernest Hemingway— *doing* things so that true sentences could be written about them—had to be conducted in public. Constantly being watched, by the world and, more disconcertingly, by himself, he was soon evading himself as systematically as Poldy evades Molly. His subject had become Ernest Hemingway and he had to keep developing the character. "How do you like it now, gentlemen?" was the false-jocose line Lillian Ross heard

him say, over and over, about his role in some unin-
teresting goings-on. The famous Style became performance, began eying itself, imitating itself. It de-
veloped formulae: flat nouns, short clauses linked by
"and." The day came when he could live with none of
this any longer.

As much as Daisy Miller, Hemingway died of the
American belief in sincerity: of believing there was
such a thing as One True Sentence. But truth is multiple, and the *whole* truth about even a circumscribed
situation is probably incommunicable. (Joyce learned
that in writing *Dubliners*; look at "Eveline" or
"Clay.") The merest beginning on the whole story of
Eveline would entail her sense of what is happening—
the story we have—and her father's, "Frank"'s, her
brother Harry's, a neighbor's, and entail them, what is
more, simultaneously. ("Simultaneously" gives us
Finnegans Wake; "serially" gives us *Ulysses*.) The True
Sentence, in Joyce's opinion, had best settle for being
true to the voice that utters it, and moreover had best
acknowledge that when voices commence listening to
themselves they turn into styles. If they don't commence listening to themselves they degenerate like the
voice of Theodore Dreiser. Style is a necessary evil.
Fortunately it can also be entertaining. "All those who
are interested in the spread of human culture among
the lower animals (and their name is legion) . . ."
[311/309]: a typical "boring" interpolation into "Cyclops." But read it in the light of Mark V, verses 8–13,
and be transported by an act of attention.

So, rooted in numerous realities including the multiple voices of Dublin gossip, styles proliferate and
take over the Bloomsday Book: styles not arbitrarily
chosen but grounded, each of them, in the texture of
Bloom's experience and that of the people who experi-

ence him. The first reason "Sirens" is a musical chapter is that Molly and Boylan at that time of day have what she and Bloom agree to speak of as an appointment to sing. The first half of "Nausicaa" has the texture of the novel in which Gerty, who can no more get out of penny romances than can Eveline, descries her Mystery Man on the Beach (and the phrase is Bloom's, who has thoughts of writing a story like that). "Oxen of the Sun" is elaborately periphrastic in accordance with its chief material, student-talk ("The young sparks, it is true, were as full of extravagancies as overgrown children" [407/404], it says about itself, more or less in the manner of Burke.) And one especially eloquent chapter is the unwritten one between "Cyclops" and "Nausicaa," the hour of Bloom's visit to the Dignams' house of mourning. This chapter's absence—Sterne would have left a blank page—corresponds to the one event of the day that Bloom doesn't want to think about at all.★

Still we may suppose that there is after all a "truth" recoverable from beneath all these surfaces, a truth the writer could put straightforwardly if he wanted to. There is not. The test is "Circe," which invites us to specify the truth we are after, and encourages us to suppose that what we want is what a cine camera and a tape recorder—inviolably "objective"—would have picked up. The rest is surely hallucination, "subjective"?

But we shall find if we try that we cannot make such a distinction.

(. . .*A hand slides over his left thigh.*)

ZOE

How's the nuts?

BLOOM

Off side. Curiously they are on the right. Heavier I suppose. One in a million my tailor, Mesias, says. [476/454]

Bloom wouldn't have said that, though what Zoe says was presumably said. Yet it's in his unmistakeable idiom. He thought it? Then he said something else. What? This is bottomless.

Or we may think we can ground the fantasies in external facts, and with negligible exceptions that cannot be done either. Or we may think we can at least recognize in the dream-material the earlier, "objective" events of the day, and examine how consciousness permutes the now-familiar données. That cannot be done with any consistency either, since fantasies we want to assign to a character will employ elements he was not aware of when they occurred, either because he wasn't present at the time or because they weren't events but narrative turns of phrase. Thus Bloom didn't see Tom Rochford's machine, which figures in one of "his" fantasies, nor was he in the room when Lenehan told the Rose of Castille riddle which figures in another. However we try to rationalize "Circe" there are elements that escape. It is the second narrator's justification and triumph, an artifact that cannot be analyzed into any save literary constituents.

"Circe" attends mostly to things that don't happen, that move beyond Objectivity altogether. Especially does this apply to what seems the climax, the apparition of Bloom's dead son Rudy while Bloom stands guard over the recumbent Stephen. This is elaborately stage-managed, a grotesque sentimental epiphany, and it never crosses Bloom's thought subsequently. For Rudy, we may deduce, does not appear to Bloom at all, to Bloom who is promptly brushing straw off Stephen and bucking him up generally in orthodox Samaritan fashion. Rudy appears to *us,* a gratuitous pantomime transformation supplied by the second narrator to resolve and terminate the episode, and to serve as notation for the empiric truth that Bloom's next thoughts are paternal ones. What could be more "objective" than a boy whom we can see, in specified costume, reading a Hebrew book? Yet no one sees him at all except ourselves, who are not there but seated in front of a book of English words.

Tommy Moore's roguish finger

Joyce in Trieste lectured on Defoe, to whom no novelist has ever been more indebted. Defoe was drawn, as in *Moll Flanders* and *Roxana,* to people who pass through roles and have multiple costumes, names, identities. By writing in the first person he himself impersonates them, his skills nearly indistinguishable from those of imposture. Defoe's knack for making us believe both his characters' feignings and the London in which they feign supplied Joyce with an ideal he kept always before him, of patient fidelity to the urban particulars that carry conviction, amid so many extravangances, that *Ulysses* is somehow grounded in the real. "He crossed under Tommy Moore's roguish finger. They did right to put him up over a urinal: meeting of the waters" [162/162]. Anyone who glances at the statue of Tom Moore, over the public urinal just to the north of Trinity College, will endorse the absolute accuracy of "roguish finger." *Ulysses* contains thousands of such observations, registered with a roguish economy of which Defoe didn't dream. And yet it breaks every rule we might derive from Defoe's practice. It declines to stick to a plausibility of surfaces, it declines the decorums of unobtrusive homespun prose. It commences as though in homage to those disciplines and proceeds to kick them to shreds.

We are now in a position to say why. Scrupulous homespun prose, the plain style of narrative fidelity, was a late and temporary invention, affirming the temporary illusion that fact and perception, event and voice, are separable. Far from delivering a final truth about things, as it seemed to do in the days when it was new, far from replacing the excrescences of rhetoric with "so many things, almost in an equal number of words," it corresponded, as Swift well understood, to

a specialized way of perceiving for specialized pur-
poses, such as recording the behavior of a cat in an
airpump. Like all specializations—Swift knew this
too, and showed he knew it when he had the Lilliputians describe Gulliver's watch—it is potentially
comic, is only kept from comedy by our agreement
that something *serious* is going forward. Rhetoric in all
its play is a human norm, the denotative plain style one
of its departments merely. To let the supernatural back
into drama, to let rhetoric and the Muse back into
fiction, these deeds of Eliot's and Joyce's were parallel
homages to a drama that began with the god-dance
and a fiction that began with Homer. Homer, the
educator of Greece, educates us still, not least when we
glimpse him in the mocking mirrors of a novel that
was not long ago thought to travesty him, but that in
fact soberly, exuberantly pays him intricate homage.

It pays him the final homage of restoring her ancient domain to the Muse. "Tell me, Muse, of that
man . . . ." The third and last part of *Ulysses,* the
homecoming, is a coming home of narrative to
the Muse. Its episodes are "Eumaeus," "Ithaca,"
"Penelope."

In "Ithaca" it is surely the "Tell me, Muse" formula
that is generating, paragraph by paragraph, the entire
chapter. One voice asks, the other imperturbably
answers.

How did they take leave, one of the other, in separation?
Standing perpendicular at the same door and on different
sides of its base, the lines of their valedictory arms meeting
at any point and forming any angle less than the sum of two
right angles.
What sound accompanied the union of their tangent, the

disunion of their (respectively) centrifugal and centripetal hands?

The sound of the peal of the hour of the night by the chime of the bells in the church of Saint George. [703–04/ 624–25]

The Muse answers tirelessly; she has geometry to impart, and metrical poetry, information about the characters' pasts and about their innermost thoughts; and she can deluge us with information we never thought to want, the acreage of the reservoirs of the Dublin waterworks or the output in candlepower of the gasflame on Bloom's kitchen range; she can rise also to a poetry of which we had not suspected the possibility, notably in the grave cadences which celebrate the domain of Odysseus, Water, for some 500 accurate ceremonious words, and conclude with "the noxiousness of its effluvia in lacustrine marshes, pestilential fens, faded flowerwater, stagnant pools in the waning moon" [672/593].

And she is also androgynous Bloom, and the questioner is also Molly, the catechism dictated by the catechetical interrogation that has recently become a habit of Molly's and is barely sketched at the episode's close. So there are gaps, there are evasions, many. The very budget—Objectivity of Objectivities—is tampered with, to delete the sum left behind in the whorehouse. For though "objective" is what we generally hear "Ithaca" called, objective is exactly what it is not. It is incomplete and only intermittently straightforward, it is confined to no one's experience, it does not adhere except whimsically to a chronology of impressions—Gulliver in Lilliput by contrast told the plain truth—and it refuses restriction to the experiences of the senses. It encompasses even Bloom's

Beatific Vision, life amid the eeltraps, lobsterpots, lawnmowers and lilactrees of Bloom Cottage, St. Leopold's, Flowerville.

Could Bloom of 7 Eccles Street forsee Bloom of Flowerville?

In loose allwool garments with Harris tweed cap, price 8/6, and useful garden boots with elastic gussets and wateringcan, planting aligned young firtrees, syringing, pruning, staking, sowing hayseed, trundling a weedladen wheelbarrow without excessive fatigue at sunset amid the scent of newmown hay, ameliorating the soil, multiplying wisdom, achieving longevity. [714–15/636]

And his coat of arms will bear "the appropriate classical motto (*Semper paratus*)" [715/636], the book's explicit acknowledgment of the epithet in the *Odyssey*'s first line, *polytropos*.

This symbiosis by dialogue of author and Muse—one asking, one answering, the hero emerging, rotated, perfected, immobilized, apotheosized—is the point of classical balance: Bloom at home, fiction likewise come home to the place whence Objectivity's siren song once lured her away. Bloom not yet at home, we have the graceless "Eumaeus": sprawling, architecturally defective alike in its plan and in the interstices of its sentences, as of Bloom himself, Museless, musing. Like *Gulliver's Travels*, incidentally, it grows curiously preoccupied with horses, and on its last page our old friend the Vivid Narrator, long mistaken by the vulgar for a connoisseur of excrement, supplies *Ulysses* with his last contribution, a few perfectly turned phrases that shine in the graceless syntax:

The horse, having reached the end of his tether, so to speak, halted, and, *rearing high a proud feathering tail*, added his quota by letting fall on the floor, which the brush would soon brush up and polish, *three smoking globes of turds. Slowly, three times, one after another, from a full crupper, he mired.* [665/585]

Farewell, old virtuoso, that was done consummately.

Then "Ithaca," the ceremonious exchange between narrator and Muse, formal, the two sharing an idiom that they have under thorough command and that permits no voices to be heard but theirs. And finally "Penelope": Muse without narrator, direct as "Eumaeus" is not, never elegantly varied but asprawl with a liquid formlessness of its own, to contrast with the "Eumaeus" formlessness which is like a heap of magpie's gatherings.

"Penelope," unpunctuated, unnarrated—the only episode with not one narrative interruption—would appear to show us how the Muse behaves without Homer: a great feminine welling of lore and opinion and gossip and feeling with (as Joyce himself said) neither beginning nor middle nor end. "a quarter after what an unearthly hour I suppose theyre just getting up in China now combing out their pigtails for the day well soon have the nuns ringing the angelus theyve nobody coming in to spoil their sleep except an odd priest or two for his night office the alarmclock next door at cockshout clattering the brains out of itself let me see if I can doze off 1 2 3 4 5 what kind of flowers are those they invented like the stars the wallpaper in Lombard street was much nicer. . ." [781/702]—it ends only when its speaker falls asleep and may not end then.

This is a voice in the dark, cut off from sensory experience save for bodily functions and the distant wail of a train: the voice of the pure composing faculty, upwelling, all-knowing: she knows everything Bloom thinks she doesn't, beginning with the contents of the drawer with the erotic postcards in it and the fact of his correspondence with Martha Clifford. "What sort of flowers are those they invented like the stars" indeed: Bloom, who goes by the name of Henry Flower, has by now been assimilated into the stars—"the heaven-tree hung with humid nightblue fruit" [698/619]—and the last surge of her monologue commences "I love flowers Id love to have the whole place swimming in roses" [781/703].

Always, whatever she tells, she tells us of that man, *polytropos*, "skilled in all ways of contriving." In her darkness the myths coalesce, amid the coalescence of all particular things, and of all men into an eponymous "him." And from the heart of the labyrinth where a Queen thanks to Dedalus' contriving has coupled with a prize bull named Blazes, the voice wells up of the eternal Ausonian Muse, readmitted to the domain of story-telling from which Objectivity thought to banish her when it shut out myth and rhetoric and supposed that the new heaven and the new earth could be bought with particulate facts sequentially dispensed like copper coins.

Supplementary Notes

(P. 9) *Flaubert's mimesis*

Elle le reconduisait toujours jusqu'à la première marche du perron. Lorsqu'on n'avait pas encore amené son cheval, elle restait là. On s'était dit adieu, on ne parlait plus; le grand air l'entourait, levant pêle-mêle les petits cheveux follets de sa nuque, ou secouant sur sa hanche les cordons de son tablier, qui se tortillaient comme des banderoles. Une fois, par un temps de dégel, l'écorce des arbres suintait dans la cour, la neige sur les couvertures des bâtiments se fondait. Elle était sur le seuil; elle alla chercher son ombrelle, elle l'ouvrit. L'ombrelle, de soie gorge-de-pigeon, que traversait le soleil, éclairait de reflets mobiles la peau blanche de sa figure. Elle souriait là-dessous à la chaleur tiède; et on entendait les gouttes d'eau, une à une, tomber sur la moire tendue.

The only personal subject to be found in these sentences is "elle"; Charles and the anonymous hind who brings round his horse are alike swallowed up by "on." Midway, three little tableaux catch the quality of his stricken rapture: "Elle était sur le seuil; elle alla chercher son ombrelle, elle l'ouvrit": a standing, a leaving, an opening, each registered with hallucinatory awe. English idiom won't accommodate such constructions without a look of faux-naif contrivance, and in not reproducing them the translator (Mildred Marmur) has rightly elected fidelity to Flaubert's preemptive concern, that we shall not hear the machinery whirring.

(P. 17) *Antonomasia of the privy*

The "outhouse" of Uncle Charles is of course an out-
door privy, concealed behind a euphemism so genteel
its cloacal connotations eluded the OED (which speaks
vaguely of "some subsidiary purpose"). In "Grace," as
we have seen, a downstairs room frequented on similar
errands is called a "lavatory" as though one merely
washed there, in consonance with the convention that
its frequenters are "gentlemen." What Bloom visits
just before 8:45 a.m. is called the "jakes," a name Joyce
seems to have chosen with one eye on his Homeric
parallels. The OED derives "jakes" from "Jaques" or
"Jack's" (cf. "john"); but we may choose to recall, in
this metempsychotical chapter, Sir John Harington's
1596 paean to the watercloset, *The Metamorphosis of
Ajax*, so entitled "because I will write of A Jakes"; still
more the anonymous rejoinder of the same year, *Ulysses Upon Ajax*, included with Harington's farrago in
the 1814 reprint Joyce may have heard of. If so, then
at the end of episode 4 behold Ulysses Visiting a
Metamorphosis of Ajax; behold rather even Ulysses
Upon Ajax for what Gerty MacDowell calls "a certain
purpose," thus to repay as it were by anticipation the
snub he will receive from the schema's "Ajax," John
Henry Menton, at the end of episode 6.

(P. 41) *Reader-traps*

Like many radical changes, this one had already occurred by the time it became noticeable. "Sirens" set
Pound's alarm jangling, but making out for sure what
is going on proves to be a major difficulty in the preceding episode, "Wandering Rocks," the prose disciplines of which seem admirably Objective.

Father Conmee, reading his office, watched a flock of muttoning clouds over Rathcoffey. His thinsocked ankles were tickled by the stubble of Clongowes field. He walked there, reading in the evening, and heard the cries of the boys' lines at their play, young cries in the quiet evening. He was their rector: his reign was mild. [224/223]

Conmee walking along Malahide road becomes Conmee walking through the stubble of Clongowes field without the least alteration of idiom or rhythm; until this episode we may not have realized how much we depended on those little alterations to signal transitions between "outer" and "inner." The reader for whom "Malahide" and "Clongowes" are no more than names on a page may not realize that Conmee's thoughts are now miles away until "in the evening" jars with the knowledge, recently imparted, that the time is only a little past three in the afternoon.

What has happened is that the narrator has become so "objective" we're deprived of helpful information. Mr. Clive Hart, the closest student of this episode's mechanics, summarizes as follows:

But the objectivity is a fraud, a deliberate trap. The narrator makes no assumptions, provides no comment. While almost everything that he says is, strictly speaking, true, there are many lies of omission, the narrator failing to provide essential connective information which we accordingly have to extrapolate for ourselves. . . . The reader is continually in danger of making false assumptions.

Elsewhere Mr. Hart speaks of "a harsh and awkward narrator whose difficult personality is the most salient thing about the chapter": an enlightening judgment since what "objectivity" is supposed to do is efface the

narrator's presence. This "harsh and awkward" being
is the one we shall be calling the Second Narrator; he is
a mutation of the Vivid Narrator we have already met.

For Mr. Hart's findings see his essay in Hart and
Hayman, *James Joyce's Ulysses*, 1974.

(P. 43) *The music of the Sirens*

"If we are to trust the schema," but the schemata—we
have two of them—were drawn up to help publicists
write articles, and are more apt to provide slogans than
insights. A Liffeyside stroll in the vicinity of the Or-
mond Hotel can afford more help. It's an area abound-
ing in miscellaneous and secondhand shops; when we
first glimpse Bloom in this episode he is gazing into
windows at "Wine's antiques" and "Carroll's dusky
battered plate" [258/256]; when we last see him he is
gazing into "Lionel Mark's antique saleshop window"
[290/289] at a candlestick, a melodeon, a picture of
Emmet speaking his last words. This is Dublin's Sar-
gasso Sea, where unassorted junk has drifted together:
brass bedsteads, statues of the Virgin, Turkish water-
pipes, fenders, footstools, patriotic engravings, things
that once had the power to summon forth feeling.

Hence, seemingly, the decor of the chapter: an
agglomeration of musical and verbal junk, some
dusty, all higgledy-piggledy on brilliant display. The
musical effects are without exception banal: the heavy
bass chords and rippling treble figures out of which a
barroom pianist can confect an accompaniment to any
song at all. The verbal effects are correspondingly obvious, woven out of sad cliché: music's sweet charms,
life's sadness, the valor of dead patriots, sounding brass
that is gold no more.

A quayside window

(P. 48) *Joyce undermining his parodies*

We can see how this works with the aid of James S. Atherton's invaluable essay†, which identifies not only the authors imitated but the actual specimens (chiefly from two anthologies, Saintsbury's *History of English Prose Rhythm*, 1912, and Peacock's *English Prose: Mandeville to Ruskin*, 1903) from which the effects were studied. Thus Macaulay writes (Saintsbury, p. 371),

> The place was worthy of such a trial. It was the great hall of William Rufus, the hall which had resounded with acclamations at the inauguration of thirty kings, the hall which had witnessed the just sentence of Bacon and the just absolution of Somers, the hall where the eloquence of Strafford had for a moment awed and melted a victorious party inflamed with just resentment, the hall where Charles had confronted the High Court of Justice with the placid courage which has half redeemed his fame. Neither military nor civil pomp was wanting. The avenues were lined with grenadiers. The streets were kept clear by cavalry. . . .

This excerpt contains the longest Macaulay sentence Saintsbury displays; Joyce took note of its habits— notably the recurrent syntactic marker, "the hall which . . . ," "the hall which . . . ," by whose aid it guides its reader through a chain of clauses in apposition—and as we shall see was careful to construct the longest sentence of his imitation on quite unmacaulay- esque principles. In the opening lines of his pastiche the original is just recognizable—

†"The Oxen of the Sun," in Hart and Hayman, *James Joyce's Ulysses: Critical Essays* (1974).

The debate which ensued was in its scope and progress an epitome of the course of life. Neither place nor council was lacking in dignity. The debaters were the keenest in the land, the theme they were engaged on the loftiest and most vital. The high hall of Horne's house had never beheld an assembly so representative and so varied nor had the old rafters of that establishment ever listened to a language so encyclopaedic. A gallant scene in truth it made. . . . [417/414]

—though "Neither place nor council was lacking in dignity" shrivels slightly in the light of "Neither military nor civil pomp was wanting" (pomp is adducible, grenadiers, cavalry; dignity is only ascribable, and may get ascribed to sententiousness or a necktie). The middle part of Joyce's version commences a systematic deviation from Macaulay's method as explicitly analyzed by Saintsbury. Macaulay's eye surveys the splendid throng:

There were seated round the Queen the fair-haired young daughters of the house of Brunswick. There the Ambassadors of great Kings and Commonwealths gazed with admiration on a spectacle which no other country in the world could present. There Siddons, in the prime of her majestic beauty, looked with emotion on a scene surpassing all the imitations of the stage. There the historian of the Roman Empire . . . .

and Saintsbury remarks, as "too obvious for comment," "the privotal, or rather spring-board, effect of the repeated 'there'," which Joyce accordingly eschews:

Crothers was there at the foot of the table in his striking Highland garb, his face glowing from the briny airs of the

Mull of Galloway. There too, opposite to him was Lynch, whose countenance bore already the stigmata of early depravity and premature wisdom. Next the Scotsman was the place assigned to Costello, the eccentric, while at his side was seated in stolid repose the squat form of Madden. . . . [417/414]

No "there" repeatedly stabs its orator's finger to guide us through the Joycean list. Macaulay, it is clear, takes every opportunity to schematize his syntax and repeat it; the "there" of the long central section of his paragraph works like "the hall which" in his one long sentence, to assure his reader that heterogeneous spectacle is controlled by brief acts of repeated predication. Joyce on the contrary does not once repeat a structure, and *his* long sentence, saved for his paragraph's end, isn't an iteration but a swaybacked marvel, constantly shifting and shuffling beneath more and more weight: Stephen and Lenehan and Bloom and voluptuous Molly:

Lastly at the head of the board was the young poet who found a refuge from his labors of pedagogy and metaphysical inquisition in the convivial atmosphere of Socratic discussion, while to right and left of him were accommodated the flippant prognosticator, fresh from the hippodrome, and that vigilant wanderer, soiled by the dust of travel and combat and stained by the mire of an indelible dishonour, but from whose steadfast and constant heart no lure or peril or threat or degradation could ever efface the image of that voluptuous loveliness which the inspired pencil of Lafayette has limned for ages yet to come. [417–18/414–15]

Little is left of Macaulay save the vigorous knowingness; it is difficult, given Saintsbury's critical pointers and Joyce's mimetic skill, to account such infidelities inadvertent.

Noting that the Dickens paragraph too does not sound really like Dickens, Mr. Atherton suggests that "Joyce's austerities in punctuation made it difficult for him to imitate Dickens who relied so heavily on the semicolon and the dash, stops that Joyce abjured." But nothing prevented Joyce from sprinkling the paragraph in question with semicolons and dashes if he had wanted to.

(P. 64) *Myth in the Odyssey*

In *The Genesis of Ezra Pound's Cantos* (1976) Ronald Bush reminds us that while the archaeological Homer who emerged toward the end of the nineteenth century displaced the Victorian Homer of noble aspect, he did not by any means preempt the field of available Homers. The Cambridge anthropologists in particular—Frazer, Jane Harrison, Tylor—gave a new meaning to the idea that the base of the *Iliad* and the *Odyssey* is not history but myth. "Myth" as they presented it no longer meant a pleasant story or an effort to explain why the seasons vary; it meant autochthonous religious rite, propitiatory, bloody.

The origins of religion interested Joyce—witness his preoccupation with Vico—and there are signs that he had read Jane Harrison's *Themis*, but it was the archaeologists' Homer he found useful for *Ulysses*, where the city's bricks, its circulating coins, its broken dishes, correspond to principal kinds of archaeological evidence. The romance of the vanished barely touched him, least of all the romance of vanished rite: Latin liturgy audible today was resonant enough: "*et unam*

sanctam catholicam ecclesiam: the slow growth and
change of rite and dogma like his own rare thoughts, a
chemistry of stars" [20–21/27].

The argument of *Themis*—I quote the useful sum-
mary of Mr. Bush—was that "Athenian customs had
their roots in fertility rites, and that the archaic Greek
heroes, whether they began as historical or legendary
figures, became important only as they acquired the
status of fertility daimons. According to *Themis*, both
rite and myth recreate the cycle of those fertility or
'eniautos' daimons 'from the cradle to the grave and
back again, to life and marriage.' The Homeric epics,
she wrote, do not mirror that cycle because they came
'late': 'Homer marks a stage when collective thinking
and magical ritual are, if not dead, at least dying'"
(p. 128).

Ezra Pound in Canto I sweeps us back into the
foretime of chanted rhythms and blood ritually spilled
to nourish ghosts, but if Joyce read *Themis* he found in
it encouragement to keep his Ulysses in the here and
now, when magical rituals (not to speak of once-
potent words, "Haec est enim calix sanguinis mei")
were dead or dying. Bloom is a murderer of fecund
Oxen, onanist and practitioner of superficial coition
("he must do it somewhere and the last time he came
on my bottom" [740/661], Molly recalls), and if we
think of him as a sometime fertility daimon it is only
to perceive with renewed force that in the here and
now he is a mere Ulysses, treading "with precaution"
paved and calibrated streets.

(P. 65) *Homeric translators*

Professor W. B. Stanford in *The Ulysses Theme* (second edition, 1964, p. 276, note 6), records the answer of

Stanislaus Joyce to his query; Stannie recalled Jim using only two translations, Cowper's and Butler's (the latter published 1900, hence the most up-to-date version available when *Ulysses* was being thought out.) Stanislaus Joyce's freedom to inspect his brother's working books must be located before the 1914 war broke out, since shortly after that Stannie was interned and Jim subsequently left for Zurich. So it seems probable that his testimony chiefly pertains to the nascent stages of Joyce's book. Frank Budgen's recollection of Joyce using Butcher and Lang comes from later years, when Joyce was studying Victorian-Homeric diction in order to parody it in "Cyclops":

And lo, as they quaffed their cup of joy, a godlike messenger came swiftly in, radiant as the eye of heaven, a comely youth, and behind him there passed an elder of noble gait and countenance, bearing the sacred scrolls of law, and with him his lady wife, a dame of peerless lineage, fairest of her race. [298/297]

This is instantly retranslated into the demotic:

Little Alf Bergan popped in round the door and hid behind Barney's snug, squeezed up with the laughing . . . . I didn't know what was up and Alf kept making signs out of the door. And begob what was it only that bloody old pantaloon Denis Breen in his bath slippers with two bloody big books tucked under his oxter and the wife hotfoot after him, unfortunate wretched woman trotting like a poodle. [298–99/297]

When (as rarely) Joyce needed to signal the presence of Homer by *stylistic* means the Butcher-Lang style was the only useful one.

(P. 68) *Invisible style*

The invisibility of the ambient style—the "schema" of E. H. Gombrich in *Art and Illusion*—explains both how fakes are possible and how they get detected. Museums apply X-rays and chemicals to suspicious objects, but what makes curators suspicious? Not long after a piece of "Etruscan" statuary at the Metropolitan had turned out to be of Victorian provenance, I heard the explanation from a museum director.

Into that object the faker had incorporated two styles, one inadvertently. His deliberate skills had gone into reproducing every Etruscan mannerism he knew. Meanwhile his nineteenth-century tastes and fingers were making an impress that was invisible the day the piece left his studio. Only the Etruscanisms could be seen, for no more then than at any other time had con-noisseurship a way to perceive the marks of its own date. But slowly men's eyes changed, and one day nothing was more evident than a Victorian sculptural schema on which Etruscan touches looked superim-posed like the wilful acts they were.

It follows, incidentally, that parody and pastiche must undergo constant change; thus late-nineteenth-century parodies of Wordsworth sound today less Wordsworthian than they sound like late-Victorian light verse, and sooner than any other part of *Ulysses*, "The Oxen of the Sun" is likely to sound like some pages written around 1920.

(P. 76) *In medias res*

Mr Leopold Bloom ate with relish the inner organs of beasts and fowls. He liked thick giblet soup, nutty gizzards, a stuffed roast heart, liver slices fried with crustcrumbs, fried hencod's roes. Most of all he liked grilled mutton kidneys, which gave to his palate a fine tang of faintly scented urine. [54–55/57]

At this first of all the Bloom paragraphs we encounter a leap in time, apparently back once more to 8 a.m. In that case, since he is not eating now, "ate" must be a frequentative verb, pertaining to what he characteristically ate.

On our second trip through the book, though, we are at liberty to remember the meal in "Sirens," and take the verbs of this paragraph as narrative past-tense specifiers of that meal. If so, time here folds briefly forward, not backward, introducing the hero as is proper *in medias res*.

And only Joyce and ourselves can savor the echo, in "faintly scented urine," of Stephen's "Dead breaths I living breathe, tread dead dust, devour a urinous offal from all dead" [50/55], which it follows in the text by a page or so but precedes in narrative time by several hours.

(P. 78) *The watch that stopped*

And if a style can create an event, can it also perhaps create a physical object, of the complexity of a watch? For there is a puzzle about this watch of Bloom's which stops so dramatically at half past four ("Was that just when he, she?" [370/367]. It may have been.) All day the hero of this time-conscious novel depends on bells and public timepieces, and except for one earlier glance at what is called "his watch" you'd have said a watch was a thing he didn't carry. Nor is that quick glance reassuringly conclusive. It occurs just after he enters Davy Byrne's: "What will I take now? He drew his watch. Let me see now. Shandygaff?" [171/171]. Nosey Flynn promptly salutes him, and later tells Davy Byrne that "If you ask him to have a drink first thing he does he outs with the watch to see what he ought to imbibe" [178/178]. But though Nosey Flynn claims to be describing a recent occurrence ("Didn't you see him look at his watch? Ah, you weren't there" [178/177–78]) he describes it askew since he certainly didn't ask Bloom to have a drink and in the Rosenbach manuscript Bloom didn't look at a watch either. The sentences at that stage read simply, "What will I take. Let me see now."

So in the incident as it stood when Joyce first thought "Lestrygonians" completed and made the Rosenbach copy, what can Nosey Flynn have been referring to? Why, to something he did see, and describes with the accuracy of most barfly descriptions: Bloom looking at a clock when Boylan is mentioned, and then sipping burgundy to quench the thought of Boylan at four.

—Ay, now I remember, Nosey Flynn said, putting his hand in his pocket to scratch his groin. Who is this was telling me? Isn't Blazes Boylan mixed up in it?

A warm shock of air heat of mustard hauched on Mr Bloom's heart. He raised his eyes and met the stare of a bilious clock. Two. Pub clock five minutes fast. Time going on. Hands moving. Two. Not yet.

His midriff yearned then upward, sank within him, yearned more longly, longingly.

Wine.

He smellsipped the cordial juice and, bidding his throat strongly to speed it, set his wineglass delicately down.

—Yes, he said. He's the organiser in point of fact.

No fear. No brains. [172–73/172]

No brains indeed: this is surely the incident Nosey reports to Davy Byrne, and what he reports, bating a gratuitous watch, is what he saw: Bloom checking the time, then drinking.

The earlier incident, when Bloom is deciding what drink to order, was amplified by the phrase "He drew his watch" for the *Little Review* publication (January 1919). It's possible that by that time the stopped watch in "Nausicaa" had crossed Joyce's mind, and that he now planted a watch to substantiate it.

Whether so or not, his interest in Bloom's watch remained slight. He not only never has Bloom consult it again, he does not have him mention it in the search of his pockets at the end of "Lestrygonians," a mere dozen pages from "He drew his watch." Bloom has just espied Boylan and improvises urgent business:

I am looking for that. Yes, that. Try all pockets. Handker. *Freeman*. Where did I? Ah, yes. Trousers. Purse. Potato. Where did I? . . .

His hand looking for the where did I put found in his hip pocket soap lotion have to call tepid paper stuck. Ah, soap there! . . . [183/183]

No watch. (Yet in "Circe," searched again—[437/430] —a pocket does yield a watch!) Nor is a watch removed from his pocket, let alone wound, during the time of divestiture in "Ithaca."

Though no omissions in *Ulysses* are conclusive, we have at least warrant for tentatively guessing that the watch Bloom draws from his pocket in "Lestrygonians" is a back-formation prompted by the style of "Nausicaa"; drawn once, looked at once, and promptly (by the author) all but forgotten.

By the way: though Bloom's "Very strange about

my watch" is followed by "Wristwatches always
going wrong" [373/371], we aren't to conclude that the
phantom watch is a wristwatch (exotic in 1904) since
when Gerty sees him "winding the watch or whatever
he was doing to it" [361/359] she also sees him "put it
back," a locution inapplicable to wristwatches.

(P. 89) Sweets of Sin *as reader-trap*

The setter of the reader-traps is of course the second
narrator, in the first episode of which he has exclusive
charge. At its exact center, immobile, this untrust-
worthy virtuoso has stationed the dark form of Mr.
Bloom, assaying and renting *Sweets of Sin.* It's for
Molly, though his criterion of choice is his own ec-
static response, and it's a way to tell her things: that he
devotedly pampers her literary tastes, that he knows
what they're both pretending has a "musical" explanation, why Boylan is coming to the house. (He opened
Sweets of Sin—*sortes Virgilianiae*—at the sentence "All
the dollarbills her husband gave her were spent in the
stores on wondrous gowns and costliest frillies. For
him! For Raoul!" [236/235] and he wants her to know
that he apprehends the analogy. It has yielded a surer
oracle than Shakespeare, whose works he has in the
past consulted "more than once for the solution of
difficult problems," obtaining however only "imper-
fect conviction.")

Sweets of Sin like any pornographic work presents
more than one reader-trap. The first, in "Wandering
Rocks," is the trap of supposing Bloom rented it solely
because he found it arousing. The second, in "Ithaca,"
presents as evasive a face as any other Bloom-Molly
communication. In the bed she questions, he replies;
then a narrative question is asked, "With what mod-

ifications did the narrator reply to this interrogation?''
[735/656] and a two-part answer is given: things he
omitted, things he included. The inclusions are mostly
falsifications, as that he went to *Leah* or dined with
Stephen at Wynn's Hotel, and among them we find "a
volume of peccaminous pornographical tendency entitled *Sweets of Sin*, anonymous, author a gentleman of
fashion" [735/656]. Stupefied by the plethora of information, we are apt to conclude that it was something he didn't mention. But no, it is an inclusion,
something he did. Then why, since he truly acquired
it, is it listed among the "modifications" of his narrative? It was added to the list subsequent to the writing-
out of the Rosenbach manuscript, and I at one time
supposed that either Joyce or the printer had inserted
it in the wrong half of the paragraph. I now think not,
since another of the positive modifications is Bloom's
"aeronautical feat"—his leap down to the areaway—
which is also true.

The trap is to suppose that "modification" means
modification of truth. But apparently it means modification of the catechetical form, for instance information Bloom volunteered that Molly didn't think to ask
for. She didn't ask how he entered without his key.
And she didn't ask if he got her another book (after
Boylan, her thirst for pornography is slaked), and his
last valiant flicker is to assert that he has it, to intend
that she shall read it, to intend that she shall guess how
much he has guessed. It is one of the pluckiest and sad-
dest details this rich book has to offer.

(P. 91) *An act of suppression*

This visit to the Dignams' was Bloom's corporal work
of mercy for the day, a troublesome and unselfish act

that ought to give him satisfaction, so we seem invited
to speculate on why he represses it from memory so
completely. All he has to say about it is in the latter part
of "Nausicaa," little more than an hour after the event:
"But Dignam's put the boots on it [the day]. Houses of
mourning so depressing because you never know.
Anyhow she wants the money. Must call to those
Scottish widows as I promised. . ." [380/378]. That
houses of mourning are depressing seems inadequate
to explain a blackout so total the topic never surfaces
again. The truth appears to be that Bloom senses he
was being used as a stereotype Jew, the ideal technician
to have at hand when one's purpose is to defraud a
moneylender on a technicality. (Dignam had assigned
his insurance as security, but since the insurers—the
"Scottish widows"—were never notified of this they
can be directed to make payment to the widow, not to
the lender.) The morality is sticky however charitable
the cause. And it was no Bloom-hater, it was the gentle
Martin Cunningham of all people, who thought to
mobilize Bloom's putative skills against "old
Shylock" [313/311]; so depressingly impossible is it,
even in the presence of good will, to escape from the
role people assign you.

Index